"This is a much-needed and exceptionally practical book, combining elegant theory with decades of practice wisdom from authors Chesner, Butté and Jones, who are leaders in their fields. This is an essential 'how-to' resource for supervisors and coaches, offering a feast of creative ideas for use in clinical and non-clinical settings."
Clark Baim, *PhD, Director, Birmingham Institute for Psychodrama, UK; Former Honorary President, British Psychodrama Association*

"Expanding the foundational work of Antony Williams on visual and active supervision, the authors of *Creative Action Methods in Supervision and Coaching* offer a practical, accessible, and versatile guide to enriching and deepening the processes of individual, group, virtual, and outdoor supervision. Just as Williams' book was gifted to me by my first supervisor, this one is destined to become part of a legacy connecting supervisors and supervisees across generations."
Craig Haen, *PhD, RDT, CGP, LCAT, AGPA-F, Training Director, The Kint Institute, USA*

"Congratulations to Anna Chesner, Céline Butté and Bryn Jones for this stimulating and delightful book on supervision, combining especially Morenian perspectives with embodied, practical and creative techniques. Professionals from the fields of psychotherapy, creative arts therapies, coaching and body psychotherapy may find abundant new stimuli for their supervision processes, following the clinical vignettes, practical examples and clear illustrations of action methods and creative techniques that can be applied in- and outside of the clinical space."
Heidrun Panhofer, *PhD, Director of the Master's Programme in Dance Movement Therapy, Department for Clinical Psychology, Autonomous University of Barcelona, Spain*

"I am delighted to be able to recommend this excellent book which is one of only a few published on Arts Therapies Supervision. The authors are tutors on the highly regarded Diploma in Creative Approaches to Supervision at the London Centre for Psychodrama and bring a wealth of both theoretical and practical knowledge to the process of supervision. They are incorporating Psychodrama into this process and are offering an original, responsible and very successful approach to the supervision of registered Arts Therapists."
Diane Waller, *OBE, MA (RCA), DPhil, Dip Psych, FRSA, Emeritus Professor of Art Psychotherapy, Goldsmiths University of London, UK; Honorary President, British Association of Art Therapists*

"The book *Creative Action Methods in Supervision and Coaching*, prepared for publication by three esteemed authors—Anna Chesner, Céline Butté and Bryn Jones—demonstrates the richness and diversity of action methods in practice. It addresses a significant need in the fields of supervision and coaching by exploring practical techniques, the roles of supervisors, and creative systems. The book broadens the scope by taking supervision practices beyond clinical settings, offering an inspiring and expansive perspective for both supervisors and supervisees."
Deniz Altınay, *Psych.M.A., President of İstanbul Psychodrama Institute, Türkiye; Lecturer in BAU Üniversity-İstanbul, Türkiye; Board Member of International Association for Group Psychotherapy and Group Processes (IAGP), Chair of IAGP Psychodrama Section, Co-Chair of the Social and Collective Traumas Committee of IAGP; Honorary Member of the Moreno Museum Association*

"This book is a unique contribution to the fast-expanding fields of supervision and coaching, with applications across diverse disciplines and areas of practice. Grounded in the well-established Creative Supervision Diploma training at the London Centre for Psychodrama, it sheds a light on the vital role of creativity, spontaneity and relational work in professional growth. Theoretical perspectives are richly balanced with practical examples, offering an accessible exploration of creative methods and techniques. *Creative Action Methods in Supervision and Coaching* is an essential resource for professionals seeking dynamic, experiential approaches to supervision and coaching."

Giorgos Tsiris, *Director of Education, Research and Creative Arts, St Columba's Hospice Care, UK; Senior Lecturer in Music Therapy, Queen Margaret University, UK*

Creative Action Methods in Supervision and Coaching

Creative Action Methods in Supervision and Coaching provides an accessible yet informative introduction to the key philosophy, theories and techniques for effective creative supervision practice. Co-authored by three experienced creative supervisors, this book investigates and answers key questions such as "What are action methods?" and "Why use creativity in supervision?" to highlight how creative supervision works and why it matters.

Guidance on best practice is supported by key research and theory within the field and demonstrated in practice by insights from supervisee contributors throughout. Divided into three distinct parts, chapters cover:

- An introduction to action methods in supervision.
- The application of creative techniques to supervision practice, highlighting adaptations to methods for groups or individuals, and in person or online.
- Supervision beyond the clinic, including non-clinical supervision with educators and creatives and guidance for supervision practice outdoors.

This book is a core reference for trained supervisors who are wishing to inject a more creative approach into their work and for those undertaking a training in clinical and process supervision who have an interest in embodied and creative interventions.

Anna Chesner is a psychotherapist, dramatherapist and co-director of the London Centre for Psychodrama, UK, which trains group and individual psychotherapists to UKCP registered level. She runs a private psychotherapy and supervision practice in London and has taught extensively in Europe and Asia.

Céline Butté is a registered dance movement psychotherapist and supervisor who works online, in the studio and outdoors. She teaches dance movement psychotherapy and supervision internationally and is a co-editor of *Embodied Approaches to Supervision: The Listening Body* (Routledge, 2023).

Bryn Jones is a registered dramatherapist and supervisor. He teaches on the MA Drama and Movement Therapy programme at the Royal Central School of Speech and Drama, University of London, UK. His clinical practice includes working with adults on an addiction therapy programme.

Creative Action Methods in Supervision and Coaching

Anna Chesner, Céline Butté and Bryn Jones

Routledge
Taylor & Francis Group

LONDON AND NEW YORK

Designed cover image: © Getty Images, Credit: oxygen

First published 2026
by Routledge
4 Park Square, Milton Park, Abingdon, Oxon OX14 4RN

and by Routledge
605 Third Avenue, New York, NY 10158

Routledge is an imprint of the Taylor & Francis Group, an informa business

For Product Safety Concerns and Information please contact our EU representative
GPSR@taylorandfrancis.com. Taylor & Francis Verlag GmbH, Kaufingerstraße 24,
80331 München, Germany.

Trademark notice: Product or corporate names may be trademarks or registered
trademarks, and are used only for identification and explanation without
intent to infringe.

Every effort has been made to contact copyright-holders. Please advise the publisher of
any errors or omissions, and these will be corrected in subsequent editions.

British Library Cataloguing-in-Publication Data
A catalogue record for this book is available from the British Library

ISBN: 978-1-032-56465-4 (hbk)
ISBN: 978-1-032-56466-1 (pbk)
ISBN: 978-1-003-43565-5 (ebk)

DOI: 10.4324/9781003435655

Typeset in Times New Roman
by Newgen Publishing UK

Contents

Acknowledgements

We would like to thank Andrea Blair for her illustrations and all the past trainees of the LCP Creative Supervision Training who have contributed to our training as much as the training has contributed to theirs.

A particular thanks to the individual supervisees, trainees and graduates whose words and reflections have been used throughout this book: Lewis Pickles, Paula Grech, Helen Yates, Stephen Mulley, 'A', Suha Al-Khayyat, Alex Cooke, Dr Jane Leach, Lizzie Palmer, Dr Ruth Allen and Davina Holmes.

We have also been supported by the spaces that we have used at the Cawley Centre, Maudsley Hospital and Family Futures.

Finally, huge thanks to the team at Routledge and particularly to Lauren Redhead for her patience, support and engagement with us. We also extend our gratitude to Tusitala Publishing and Jessica Kingsley Publishers for their kind permission to reuse some of the material from previous publications.

Introduction

Anna Chesner, Céline Butté and Bryn Jones

After many years of running the London Centre for Psychodrama (LCP) Creative Supervision Diploma training we felt the need to expand on and update our thinking around the approach and methods described initially in *Creative Supervision across Modalities* (Chesner and Zografou, 2014).

We have two intentions with this book. Firstly, it will serve as a more comprehensive companion to the annual training in supervision at LCP. We have addressed and developed both theoretical and practical aspects of the practice of creative supervision as described in the earlier text.

Our second intention is to widen the audience to these approaches and methods. Supervisors who have trained elsewhere may add value and variety to their supervision practice by engaging with this body of work. We have also included the word 'coaching' in our title. Whilst none of us identifies professionally as a coach we all work in non-clinical as well as clinical contexts and our hope is to invite the reflective coaching community to engage with the focused reflective approaches described in this book. Indeed, our training cohorts frequently include coaches and those trained both as coach and as counsellor or psychotherapist. We understand the main aim of coaching to be the facilitation of a client's personal or professional development by empowering them to achieve desired agreed outcomes and to maximise their potential. There is considerable crossover here with the goals of clinical and non-clinical supervision. The creative supervision model aligns with a coaching approach in the sense that the arc of a session includes finding a focus and goal for the session, a targeted piece of work on this focus, and a final piece of reflection around takeaways and next steps. As coach and sociodramatist Valerie Monti Holland writes: "Both coaching and Morenian methods stipulate a contract as the frame that holds the relationship between a coach and a client and against which any progress or scope of work is measured" (Monti Holland, 2024: 68).

We begin in Part I with theory, around the Morenian underpinnings of our approach, centred in creativity, spontaneity and relationship. We highlight the importance of warmup as a principle underpinning spontaneity and creativity. We include an integrative theory of supervision. This is based on well-established supervision theories, with some additions of our own. We emphasise the practice of working explicitly with a supervisory enquiry or focus.

DOI: 10.4324/9781003435655-1

In Part II we describe the supervisory techniques which are taught on the course and which are based in creative action methods as applied specifically to the supervisory and reflective frame. These include projective methods such as Small World concretisation, Psychodramatic approaches including Role Work and Doubling, paper-based techniques, such as Six Shape Supervision Structure, and Mandala, embodied and ritual techniques such as Four Elements and the Framework for the Embodied Reflective Narrative, and the image-based technique of the Seven Step Relationship Sequence. Each of the methods in Part II has been honed and refined over the years, both in supervision practice and within the training itself. We also include two chapters specifically on supervision for groups and teams, as well as making reference to considerations when using some of the other techniques in group settings.

In Part III we attend particularly to the wider field. With the help of colleagues whom we supervise or who have completed the training and are themselves actively supervising and/or training others we give examples of creative supervision beyond the consulting room. Settings for this work include education, third-sector institutions, theatre and community engagement, leadership and, interestingly, the world of theology and theological education within and beyond the UK. We are grateful to our colleagues for their conversations and testimony. Finally, also in Part III we include a chapter on outdoor supervision practice. While this area of work is less honed than the techniques explored in Part II, we are keen to open the doors to consider the benefits and challenges of moving beyond the consulting room in a physical as well as metaphorical sense. We are mindful of the fact that clinical, reflective and other practices are continually evolving and expanding their frames, including in the direction of working with the natural environment.

A note about inclusivity and adaptability. During the COVID-19 pandemic we had to move the training online partway through one cohort and for the entirety of the next cohort of trainees. We were delighted to find that all the action methods that we had been practising in person could be adapted to online work. We recognise that the online frame has become a preferred practical option for many supervisors and supervisees. With this in mind, we have referenced adaptations for online work throughout Part II of the book. The importance of online practice is also reflected in the training itself. We have continued to teach the Friday evening session of our monthly weekends via a virtual platform. This gives us an opportunity to address the specific considerations and adaptations necessary for safe, clear and boundaried online work.

In response to expressions of interest from practitioners overseas who are unable to attend our London-based training we now provide an online version of the course. This training enables a wider international and cross-cultural community to access the principles and methods we teach and to apply them both in person and online. In addition, the coming together of practitioners across national boundaries and practice cultures continues to stimulate our reflections on difference, inclusivity and adaptability.

Each year we are privileged to celebrate and learn from each other and our trainees in the light of the full range of differences they bring with them – practice modalities and settings, levels of experience and age, abilities and learning styles, cultures, ethnicities, and diversity in terms of sexuality, gender and other identifications. The encounters across difference that this diversity necessitates are part of the rich and deep ongoing learning for each cohort and for the staff team. Practical sociometric approaches to addressing this aspect of identity and group are unpacked in Chapter 2.

In writing this book we have mirrored our approach to delivering and developing the training, in that we have been collaborative and in dialogue throughout. Specific chapters are credited to their main authors, but in each case are the product of conversation and shared critical thinking and creative reflection. We are delighted to have on board Andrea Blair who has created the illustrations throughout. Like Céline and Bryn, she is a graduate of the training herself, as well as being an educator and arts psychotherapist. She initially worked with Anna on *One-to-One Psychodrama Psychotherapy, Applications and Technique* (Chesner, 2019). Her contributions fit with the Morenian axiom, "Show me, don't tell me!" at the heart of the psychodrama and action methods approach. We are grateful to her for the visual aids in this current text.

References

Chesner, A., 2019. *One to One Psychodrama Psychotherapy, Applications and Technique*. Routledge.

Chesner, A., and Zografou, L., 2014. *Creative Supervision across Modalities*. Jessica Kingsley Publishers.

Monti Holland, V., 2024. "Dressing for the Occasion, Using Morenian Methods and Presence in Coaching to Cultivate Agency". In *Psychodrama und Soziometrie*, 23, p. 63–75. https://doi.org/10.1007/s11620-024-00834-z. Accessed 30 May 2025.

Part I

An Introduction to Action Methods in Supervision

Chapter 1

Creativity, Spontaneity and Relationship

A Morenian Perspective

Anna Chesner

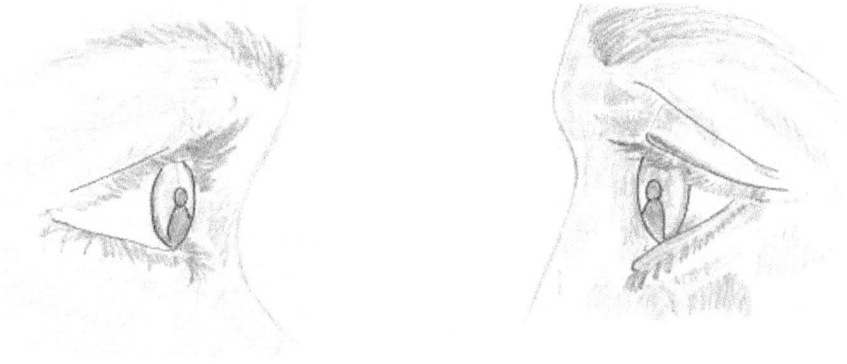

Figure 1.0

The LCP approach to creative supervision is underpinned by Moreno's philosophy. J.L. Moreno (1889–1974) was the founder of psychodrama, sociodrama, sociometry and group psychotherapy and his work was refined and expanded by his wife and collaborator Zerka T. Moreno (1917–2016). At the core of their innovative spirit was a philosophical vision that valued relationship, a vision of human beings as inherently social, and with the capacity for being creative and spontaneous.

This chapter introduces the reader to some key Morenian concepts which support the philosophy of creative supervision.

As Fox summarises (Fox, 2008: 3) Moreno believed in the value of living authentically, the importance of subjective reality, the possibility and desirability of an authentic encounter between people, and an egalitarian view of society. Moreno's famous expressionistic poem from the early twentieth century speaks vividly of the power of an authentic encounter. We might usefully consider it in terms of the potential quality of the interpersonal encounter in both therapy and supervision:

A meeting of two: eye to eye, face to face.

DOI: 10.4324/9781003435655-3

And when you are near I will tear your eyes out
and place them instead of mine,
and you will tear my eyes out
and will place them instead of yours,
then I will look at you with your eyes …
and you will look at me with mine.

(From *Invitation to an Encounter*, 1914,
quoted in Fox, 2008, p. 4, used with permission)

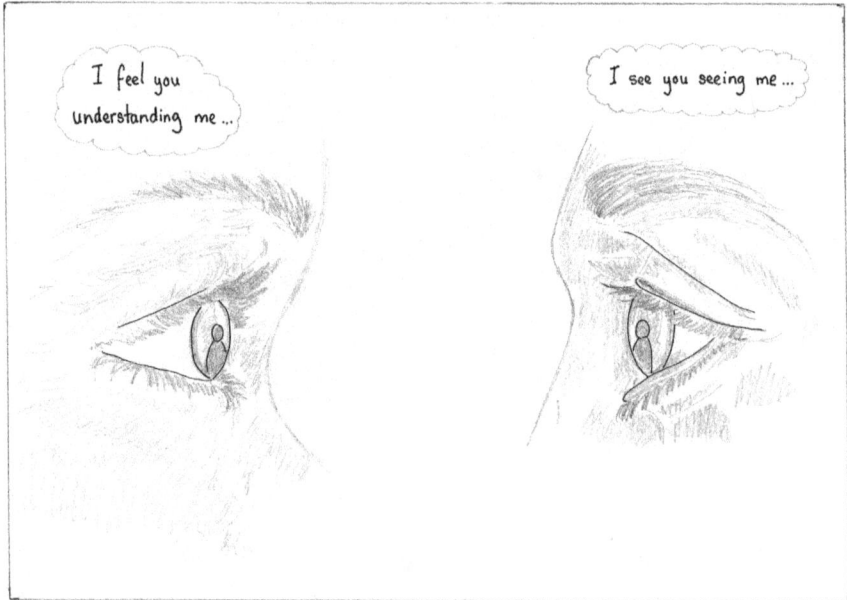

Figure 1.1 Invitation to an Encounter

Does supervision offer us the opportunity for an encounter? Yes, an encounter between two or more practitioners, whose professional and life experiences, being different, will inevitably stimulate new points of view. Furthermore, it offers us an encounter with the professional material that is being thought about, an opportunity to engage with the content and quality of the therapy, coaching or other professional work interaction in a fresh and surprising way; and an encounter with the personal–professional interface of the practitioner as it arises authentically in the work.

As proponents of creative supervision, it is important to consider what creativity is and how it relates to spontaneity. For Moreno the value of creativity relates to our cosmic nature. He was interested in the parallel between god-as-creator and man-as-creator. I have written elsewhere (Chesner, 2019) about this Promethean vision. The Greeks too were fascinated by the relationship between divine and human creativity.

As a child of four, Moreno's creative imagination was so intense that it ended up costing him a broken arm whilst playing with other children from the neighbourhood. They built a version of heaven and earth, piling chairs on a large table, high enough to reach the basement ceiling. In the role of God, he climbed to the top and his friends, in the role of angels, circled around him, encouraging him to fly. He launched himself and inevitably gravity took its toll (Nolte, 2020: 156). This experience provided a lesson in the nature of creative imagination. What we imagine has a reality, but it is a reality of the 'as if' and is not the same as the physical reality of the material world. Creative supervision embraces opportunities to work and play with the 'as if' and to allow insights gained from this endeavour to transform our clinical and professional work – without losing touch with the difference between the world of the creative imagination and the reality principle.

In psychodramatic thought creativity grows from the moment and is dependent upon a good degree of spontaneity. Spontaneity is defined as "an adequate response to a new situation or a new response to an old situation". (Moreno, 1978: 42).

When we lack spontaneity, we are limited by habit and by personal or social "cultural conserves" (Moreno, 1978: 46). Like jam these are set, congealed patterns of thinking or doing that have the characteristic of being preserved. These patterns are familiar, easy to take off the shelf, but lack the element of freshness that is the mark of creativity. For Moreno spontaneity arouses creativity, may even revitalise a habitual cultural conserve or lead to the creation of something new. It is not the same as impulsivity, which is unlikely to be "an adequate response to a new situation or a new response to an old situation". Impulsivity might arise from an instinctual and unreflective response to a personal desire (coming from the id) whereas spontaneity is mediated by a moment of reflection or awareness that relates the impulse to the current context, i.e. the moment at hand or, as Moreno defines it the old or new "situation".

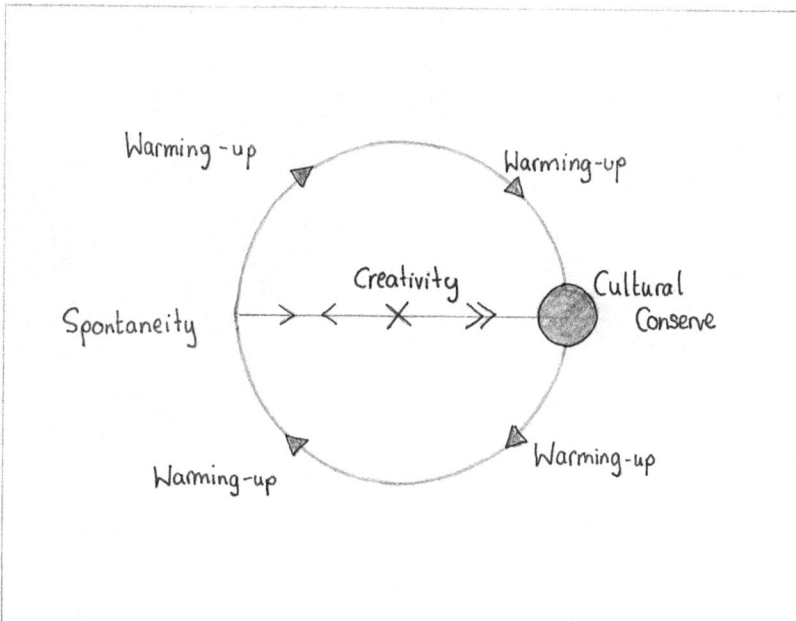

Figure 1.2 Moreno's Canon of Creativity

What does this mean for our professional lives and for creative supervision? Firstly, it is important to recognise that our ways of engaging in psychotherapy, counselling, coaching and other work are likely to become habitual. To some extent, as with all cultural conserves, this will have benefits. If we thought consciously about every small decision we make whilst driving, or whilst conducting a professional conversation, we would be re-inventing the wheel on a regular basis. On the other hand, operating too much on the basis of habitual assumptions in our professional life can lead to stagnation, a lack of surprise and a lack of openness to the creative possibilities of the moment. As Koch, Caldwell and Fuchs write about procedural memory and habitual ways of being "What we have forgotten has become what we are" (Koch et al., 2013: 13). For better or for worse we engage procedural memory and develop a style of which we lose conscious awareness.

This is where creative approaches can loosen our clients' and our own perceptions and add new perspectives to our reflections on our work. This in turn opens the door to embodying new ways of understanding and new ways of being in our work.

Holding these underpinning theoretical and philosophical perspectives in mind, let us now move forward to explore the principles of warmup, some relevant supervision theory, and numerous creative approaches to supervision.

References

Chesner, A., 2019. *One to One Psychodrama Psychotherapy*. Routledge.

Fox, J. (ed.), 2008. *The Essential Moreno: Writings on Psychodrama, Group Method, and Spontaneity by J. L. Moreno, MD*. Tusitala Publishing.

Koch, S.C., Caldwell, C., and Fuchs, T., 2013. "On Body Memory and Embodied Therapy". *Body, Movement and Dance in Psychotherapy*, 8(2), 82–94. https://doi.org/10.1080/17432979.2013.775968

Moreno, J.L., 1978. *Who Shall Survive?* Beacon House.

Nolte, J., 2020. *J.L. Moreno and the Psychodramatic Method*. Routledge.

Chapter 2

Warmup as Process and Activity

Anna Chesner

Figure 2.0

In the spontaneity–creativity cycle described in Chapter 1 the driving force towards creativity is the warmup. It is the process of preparation towards spontaneity and away from cultural conserve. Those active in the worlds of performance and sports take for granted the importance of warming up. In the context of psychotherapy, coaching and supervision warmup includes different dimensions of preparation towards being in the moment: physical, interpersonal, social and intrapsychic. The warmup provides a crucial foundation to any activity. Later chapters include descriptions of the warmup process to various creative supervision techniques as well as to the different stages within a supervision session.

Warmup is both a process and an activity. We can warm up to something without doing specific external actions. It might be a more internal process of intention or incubation of an idea. In this chapter we explore the process of warming a group up to being a supervision training group and to the use of creative action methods as a

DOI: 10.4324/9781003435655-4

shared language for learning and supervising. The activities we use are transferable to other group or individual training, supervision and practice settings. We include the Morenian process of sociometry as a distinct approach. As with a number of Morenian action methods, sociometry may be familiar from other fields, where it has been adopted as a technique without always referencing its origins.

Warming Up To Being a Training Group

What happens when a group comes together in preparation for a learning process that will last for a year? Whenever we meet a new group of people there is a need to establish safety. Each individual will arrive with their own fantasies about self as a group member, about the nature of groups, especially learning groups, and about the potential dangers of being in a group.

> Will I be seen? Will I be liked? Will there be space for me? Will there be someone who dominates or is looking for conflict? Will I be clever enough? How do I need to be, in order to be a group member? Can I belong? If I belong, will I disappear? Am I a fraud? Is everyone else better qualified, more experienced or more likeable than me?

These are just some of the anxious background thoughts that may be going on in relation to self and peers, let alone in relation to the authority figures of the training staff.

> Do I need to impress them? What do I need to do to stay invisible? What do I need to do to be seen? Will they see through me? How might they use or abuse their power and authority?

Inevitably such anxious thoughts impede spontaneity and creativity and if unaddressed get in the way of learning.

A group is a powerful entity, and it is not surprising that the first meeting can feel very charged for some group members. There may be a 'transference of situation', evoking the anxiety of a first day at school, college or university or any new beginning in the context of other people. Fortunately, a group can also be a place of safety where we can be resourced and supported. Through appropriate choice of simple shared activities, a group can activate positive social engagement that fosters emotional co-regulation and the development of safety (see Porges, 2017). In this way, we can use warmup activities to facilitate a process of warming up to presence, collaboration, connection, spontaneity and ease.

Sociometry as Warmup Activity

The way that we approach the start of the training models something quite important about beginnings and foundations. It has particular relevance to group supervision (see Chapter 6) but also to the beginnings and warming-up process vital to all supervisory, coaching and educative relationships. For this reason, we describe some of the activities we have developed in detail, starting with sociometry.

We begin by making a circle and collectively ensure that everyone in the circle can make eye contact with everyone else. A circle is an egalitarian structure, and one in which the trainers are equal to the trainees. Sociometry makes visible the points of connection and difference in a group. As a method it involves using the dimension of space in the room, and the physical activity of stepping forward, or stepping back to mark who is who and where there are commonalities and differences to be acknowledged. In contrast to a common group cultural conserve of sitting and listening to each person introducing themselves one by one, sociometry bypasses what can be an agonising process of waiting, wondering what I will say, and consequently not really taking in what others are saying. In sociometry each unit of communication can be non-verbal and immediate, allowing each person to choose how much to disclose or talk about, and to do so briefly. The physicality of the exercise also helps to regulate the physical aspects of anxiety.

trainer and trainees

Figure 2.1 Sociometry–Warming Up

Here are some sample structures using sociometry. We invite the reader to consider the impact of the sequence of activities in the light of your own experience of beginnings.

Sociometry Around Pre-Existing Relationships

"If you already know someone in this room from another setting, step forward and put your hand on their shoulder". This demystifies what might have been the source of anxious fantasies, making sense of why some people seem to know each other already and minimising the paranoid fantasy of "everyone knows each other except me, I am the only outsider". Each grouping can briefly say how they already know each other; for example, we trained together and we work in the same organisation. That unit of communication being complete, they can then step back into the circle.

Sociometry Around Professional Identities

These questions offer the opportunity for group members to step in multiple times to share something of their working background and experience, whilst establishing commonalities and the reassurance of having been seen and heard in the complexity of their multiple experiences.

"Step forward if you identify with the following statements."
I work in the NHS/private practice/as a freelancer/in an educational establishment/for another kind of organisation; I work predominantly with adults/young people/children and families/managers; I identify myself as a psychotherapist/arts therapist/coach/counsellor/consultant/other.

Sociometry Around Supervision Experience

I have experience as a supervisor.
I have experience as a supervisee.
I have experience of being supervised in a group setting.
I have experience of being supervised in an individual setting.
I have more than one supervisor.

Sociometry Around Here-and-Now Feelings and Fantasies

By this point group members will have a sense of the kind of simple 'I statement' that acts as an invitation to others to share identifications. They are invited to step forward and make a simple and short statement about how they are feeling about being here. The kind of statements that may come are "I am feeling excited/anxious/relieved". We invite those who step in to say a little more about the context – "excited because, anxious because etc. … " Again, these units of communication are short, not starting points for longer conversations or monologues but ways of allowing the authentic experience of the here and now to be acknowledged and accepted in the group.

Sociometry of Personal Disclosure

Having started with the more distanced aspect of professional factors and having moved gradually towards the acknowledgement of feeling, we now give space to statements about personal factors that may helpfully be named, in order for the individual to be more authentically present. The structure for this is given by the facilitator, "Step forward with an I statement that is true for you and others can join you if they identify with that statement". The content is led by group members. The kind of material that is disclosed tends to relate to background, identity, learning style or needs and current personal circumstances. It is a consensual process, whereby each person chooses how they identify themselves and can expand a little on what they are sharing once the grouping in the middle has become clear. There is an important balance to be struck in this process. It is vital to have the chance to be seen in our differences, those that are immediately visible or audible, those that are implicitly evident, and those that are invisible but subjectively significant. Indeed, there may be quite practical considerations that need to be negotiated in response to what is shared. On the other hand, group members have the right not to have to 'represent' their class, ethnicity, culture, gender, disability, age or any other grouping. If it feels burdensome to step into the space of a particular label, that sensitivity also needs to be respected.

Where someone is the only one with a particular difference it can be useful to acknowledge this, even if it is stating the obvious, such as being the only male, or the only wheelchair user. On other occasions invisible commonalities may emerge through the identification of less obvious disabilities and the assumption of being the only one is undercut by this process. The exercise is not about forcing anything but creating an openness to acknowledge points of difference that exist within the group and that connect to wider societal factors, including power differentials. It illuminates intersectional connections and provides opportunities for conversations that may otherwise remain as unspoken elephants in the room. This is particularly important at the beginning of the process of training, in order to support an inclusive and curious culture within the learning group. We are warming up to that inclusivity and curiosity.

Notes for Facilitation of Sociometry: Group members should be guided to keep statements short and simple and beginning with the word 'I'. This may involve the facilitator holding the boundary of the structure and coaching what is a simple statement. "I work with children and adolescents in the voluntary sector" is a statement that could exclude the commonality of working with children and adolescents for those who work in private practice with that client group. "I work with children and adolescents" would be an adequate simple statement, as would "I work in the voluntary sector." "I am a mother of a three-year-old daughter and a five-year-old son" is unlikely to create a precise resonance, whilst other group members might also have the experience of parenthood. "I am a parent", "I am a mother" and "I care for two children" would all be simple statements that could elicit a clear identification or not from group members. The facilitator of sociometry may need to be more directive than they are used to. With all action methods there is a directive element to the structure, whilst the content is group, trainee or supervisee led. The exercise models this form of facilitation – playful but clear and hygienic in terms of structure.

Warming Up To Being Learners

Having begun to form as a group through sociometric introductions the group is tasked to consider what values and norms will support them in their learning together.

The question we pose is "What conditions do you need in order for this training to be a safe and productive space for your developmental process as a supervisor?" The question is explored in small groups, without intervention from the staff team. This encourages everyone to make a contribution initially within the less exposing forum of a small group, before coming together as a whole group to distil and potentially modify the final working contract. If the staff team feels that something essential has been missed, we will offer it for their consideration, but fundamentally the learning contract is created and decided by the trainee group.

We have been struck by how variable the elements of the contract are from year to year and cohort to cohort. In one year there may be a focus on the importance of having permission to not know or to 'fail' during the learning process; another year might emphasise the importance of boundaries around the purpose of the group as a training group and not a therapy group.

Warming Up to the Topic of Supervision

In this section we introduce two methods through which the group collaborates to warm up to the theme of supervision.

Stakeholder Sculpt

A key early exercise for the group is to create a supervisory stakeholder sculpt. This experiential group task addresses the question, "Who cares about supervision, to whom does it matter and in what way?"

We begin with placing two chairs into the centre of the space, quite close to each other and at a relational or conversational angle. One represents the supervisee and one represents the supervisor. This reflects the apparent simplicity of the supervisory system in its bare form. The group is then asked who else is involved and in what way. For each role that the group identifies a chair is placed in relation to the chairs/roles already identified and clearly named. Typically, roles which emerge are:

The client
The client's family
The client's community
The supervisee's family

The supervisee's accrediting body
The supervisee's setting where the work takes place
The supervisor's supervisor
The supervisor's family
The supervisor's accrediting body
Funding bodies
Training organisations
Wider professional systems (e.g. a client's social worker or colleague)
Policymakers
Wider public

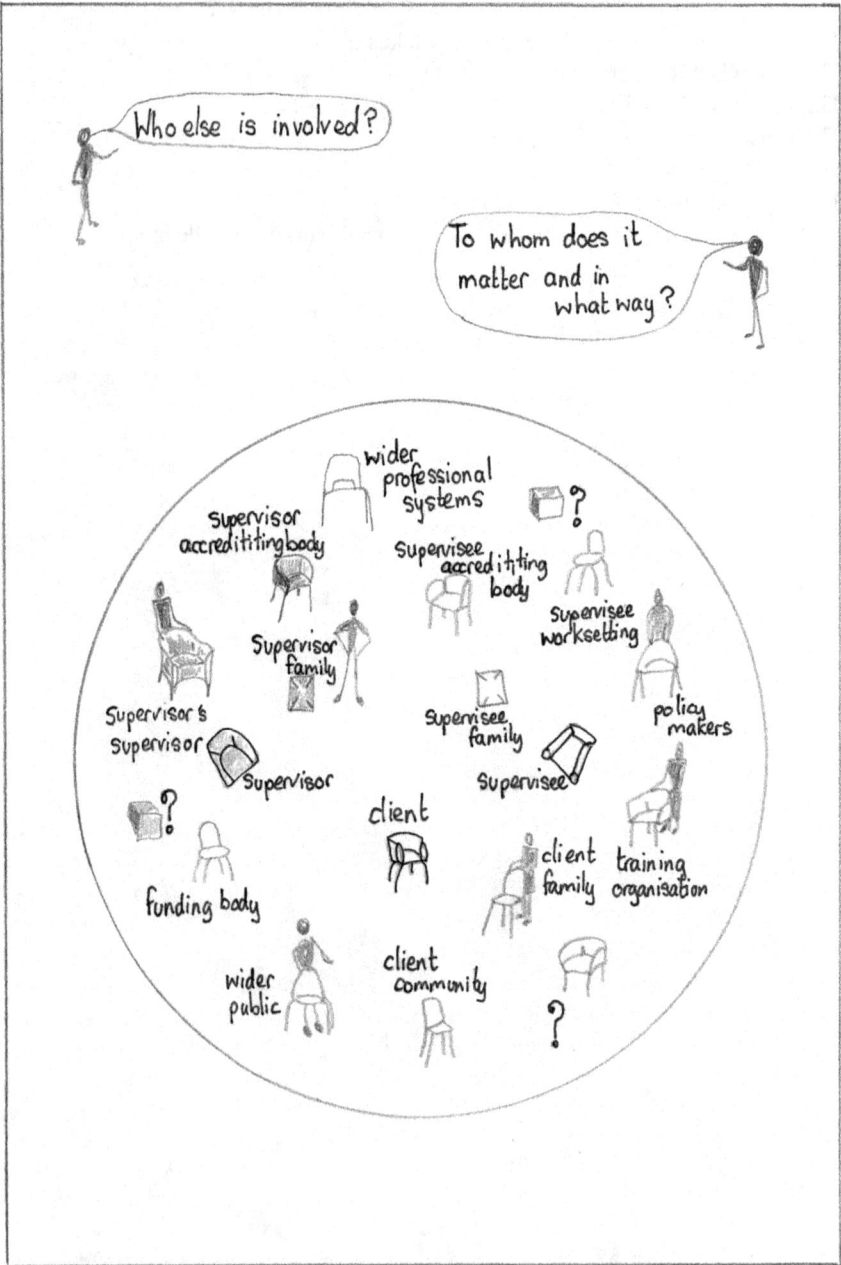

Figure 2.2 Stakeholder Sculpt 1

Once the sculpt is finished we remind ourselves of which roles are represented and where they are, and each group member sits on a chair of choice in order to explore inhabiting that role and making a brief statement from that perspective. It is not a free improvisation, insofar as the statements are relatively succinct, and we ensure that all roles are heard, but it does start to highlight lines of tension and affiliation and specific role concerns within the system. It also demonstrates powerfully how complex and extensive the wider system of therapy, coaching and supervision is.

Once this first sculpt has been brought to life in this way there is the opportunity for each group member to inhabit a new role, perhaps one that is harder to identify with. In this second round of the stakeholder interaction the hidden and conflictual dynamics often appear more explicitly. An employer that claims to value supervision in order to support the workforce may in a second round be portrayed as an employer who wants to pay lip service to supervision but fundamentally wants more client hours delivered, for example. The consideration of value for money may be more dominant than it initially appeared. Bringing the more shadowy elements of the system to light tends to be energising for the group. The dynamic is dramatic, and having inhabited it from different perspectives allows for a fuller understanding of the system.

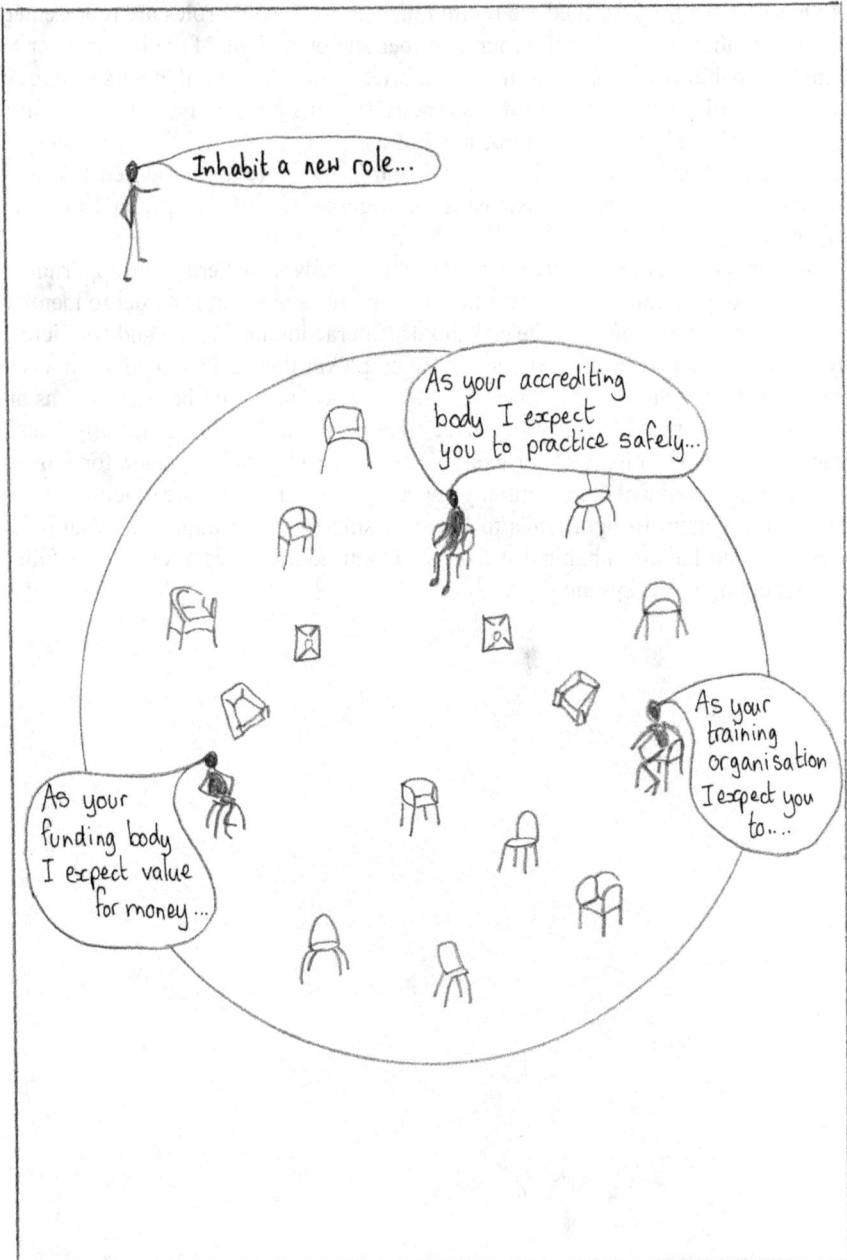

Figure 2.3 Stakeholder Sculpt 2

Warming Up to the Implicit and Explicit Expectations in the Supervisory Relationship

This activity is conducted in two parts.

Round 1: *Supervisee expectations towards supervisor*
As in the above exercise we begin with the placing of two chairs. This time how-ever they are placed at a considerable distance from each other and facing each other directly. One represents the supervisor, and the other the supervisee. To begin with the chairs are empty and a pile of props is available to the side. The group is asked initially to imagine themselves as the supervisee looking towards the supervisor and experiencing the expectations, wants and needs that are familiar to this role and that they may hold or expect others to hold towards the super-visor. One at a time each member of the group who is inspired to do so picks a prop, stands behind the supervisee chair, looks towards the supervisor and finds a place along the invisible line between the two chairs to place their prop, whilst naming to the supervisor what they expect, want or need. For example, "I need you to hold me to account", or "I expect you to know more than me". The needs, wants and expectations are not censored. Indeed, on reflection some may be quite unrealistic, for example, "I want you to give me all the answers". The rest of the group are engaged as active witnesses to this unfolding drama. Meanwhile one of the staff team is making a list on a flipchart sheet of all the expectations. When sufficient expectations have been marked there is an invitation for someone to sit on the supervisor's chair, on behalf of all of us (in the spirit of Everyman or Everysupervisor) and for someone else to sit on the supervisee chair and read out/ name all the expectations, wishes and needs that have been gathered. As in the initial gathering of these statements this phase is conducted in the first or second person. "As your supervisee I expect you to … "

We then hear role feedback from the person in role as Everysupervisor. How does it feel to be on the receiving end of these role demands? The rest of the group joins in with this reflection through their identification with the role.

It may feel daunting or exciting to be on the receiving end of the statements.

The line of props is deroled, each person removing the props they were respon-sible for laying down.

Round 2: *Supervisor expectations to supervisee*
The exercise is repeated from the other perspective, that of the supervisor. "What do we expect, want and need from supervisees?"

The same process unfolds from this differing perspective, helped by the feeling response of having heard the expectations of the supervisees.

At the conclusion of this phase of the exercise group members again occupy the seats of supervisor and supervisee and we hear the supervisor's role demands voiced to the supervisee and how these land with the person in role as supervisee.

After deroling the props and the chairs, there is space for a group reflection on which role demands are reasonable, achievable, appropriate and inappropriate.

Figure 2.4 Supervisor Supervisee Expectations

The exercise warms people up to the new role of supervisor and the new role relationship of supervisor–supervisee from the supervisor's perspective, which needs to include the supervisee's perspective. At this juncture in the training, it also connects individual trainees to their own experience of supervision, how they have used it, and to what extent their own expectations are being met. It is a warmup to their reflective and critical faculty.

In addition, it opens up the question of how supervisory relationships are contracted for and what elements the neophyte supervisor wants to include in their agreement or formal contract with a supervisee. This crucial administrative task that takes place at the start of each supervision relationship is worthy of an extensive warmup process and the exercises described so far in this chapter serve to set what could be seen as a dry necessity into the context of relationship, encounter and a wider systemic perspective.

Warming Up to the Moment, and the Moments Between Moments

During the intense process of a learning weekend, it is to be expected that there will be moments of fullness, emotional reaction and learning challenges. We apply the notion of warming up to spontaneity in order to clear the air, change the energy and give maximum opportunity for trainees to shift from one state to another, which requires a new focus.

We consider these activities as *warmup snacks* or energy regulators. These are used judiciously by the trainers according to the perceived needs and requirements of a specific group at a specific moment. Frequently they are invented in the moment, in response to what we see and feel. We tend to draw on a repertoire of breathing and movement interventions, or games that activate fun and social connection. Sometimes it is important to facilitate a re-centring of the group's attention. At other times it might be appropriate to mark a transition from one activity to another in the spirit of punctuation. Even pausing for a moment can be considered a warmup to the next moment; a time to digest and re-calibrate before stepping into a new activity or way of being. As such we consider warmup to be a central and continuous feature of our approach to training.

Warming Up To What?

Warmup activities have a playful element to them; they nurture the development of personal qualities or Roles which are indispensable to having a productive experience of the training, as well as to being a versatile creative supervisor. Traditionally in psychodramatic terms Role is the term used to describe a way of being. It comprises both a verb and a descriptor. See Chapter 5 for more on the concept of role. Here are some of the roles we encourage our trainees to warm up to and to develop:

Attuned listener
Clear and self-aware communicator
Active contributor
Embodied self-presenter
Considered responder
Collaborative participant

Conclusion

In this chapter we have introduced the concept of warmup as a key process in Moreno's spontaneity–creativity cycle. We have introduced a number of warmup activities that create a helpful learning environment in the training course and that can be easily adapted to other experiential and training groups where the work of the group relies on trust and a good level of interpersonal ease amongst participants. These include contracting for the purpose of the group and sociometry in a number of forms. Finally, we have shared some exercises with the specific task of warming up to the theme of supervision, locating supervision within the context of a wider system and reflecting on the role expectations between supervisor and supervisee and between fellow participants on the training course.

Reference

Porges, S., 2017. *The Pocket Guide to the Polyvagal Theory* W.W. Norton and Co.

Chapter 3

An Integrative Theory of Supervision

Anna Chesner

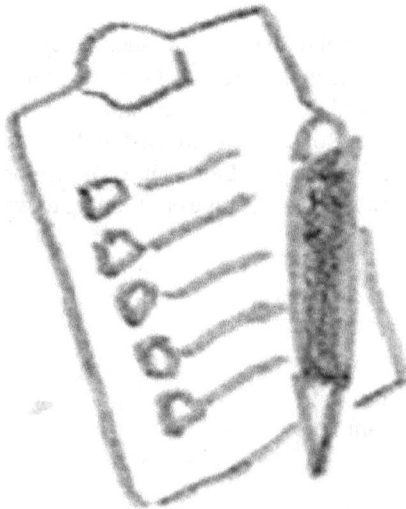

Figure 3.0

This chapter positions creative supervision within the historical context of supervision and briefly summarises some core concepts and theories, which underpin the various creative approaches described in Part II of the book.

The History of Supervision and the Place of Creative Supervision

Supervision as a practice is now a century old, and there have been a number of significant developments which parallel changes in psychotherapy, education and training. These developments have been succinctly summarised by Basa (Basa, 2017). She identifies three broad phases, summarised here.

DOI: 10.4324/9781003435655-5

The first phase, the psychoanalytic/psychotherapy model, grew out of psycho-analysis and understood the supervisory relationship to be very much like the thera-peutic relationship. At this time, in the 1920s the role of the supervisor was that of a more experienced analyst who could advise and be a role model.

The second phase, which emerged in the 1950s, reflected the different approaches to psychotherapy and to counselling which came to prominence at that time. These include cognitive behavioural, psychodynamic, person-centred and narrative approaches to supervision. Elements of the earlier phase were retained, such as reflecting on transference, countertransference and defence mechanisms.

The third phase she identifies as starting in the 1970s and is characterised by a more developmental or educational approach to the task of supervision, as opposed to a psychotherapeutic or counselling one. Supervision is seen as a place to reflect, and the process includes experiential processes and systemic perspectives. It includes process, function and competency models.

Creative Supervision acknowledges its roots in each of these three phases and is largely informed by the developments in the 1970s. We draw in particular on the developmental learning aspect of the Integrative Developmental Model (IDM) framework (Stoltenberg and McNeill, 2010), the Seven Eyed/double matrix pro-cess model of Hawkins and Shohet (Hawkins and Shohet, 2012) and Inskipp and Proctor's (1993) formative, normative and restorative task and function model of supervision.

Antony Williams (1995) seems to be a pioneer in writing about Visual and Active Supervision. We have extended his systemic/psychodramatic approach to a broader foundation of creative approaches to supervision. We are interested in approaches which go beyond words in helping the supervisee access knowing and reflection through the body and the imagination whilst maintaining a rigorous theoretical base, informed by the contributions of the theoreticians and practitioners named above.

The key elements of our theoretical base are presented here in summary. Following chapters draw on these concepts and illustrate their use in relation to specific supervision vignettes.

The Supervisory Question or Focus

A supervisory enquiry benefits from being honed and made precise. It forms a mini-contract that ensures that the reflective enquiry being addressed meets the curiosity and need of the supervisee. Establishing a supervisory question/focus/ enquiry is a relational moment – an opportunity for alignment and collaboration. It is also an aesthetic moment, a shared beginning, which creates the starting point of an arc of inquiry – either for the whole session or for a part of a session. The hon-ing and clarifying of the supervisory question functions as a warmup to the role of reflective practitioner and succinct communicator early on in the session.

The Five Roles of the Supervisor

We have identified five key roles or ways of being that the supervisor inhabits at different moments of the supervisory process. These are Administrator, Teacher, Facilitator, Consultant and Evaluator. The latter four of these draw heavily on the supervisory roles as described by Williams (1995). The first is something identified by Chesner in the context of this training.

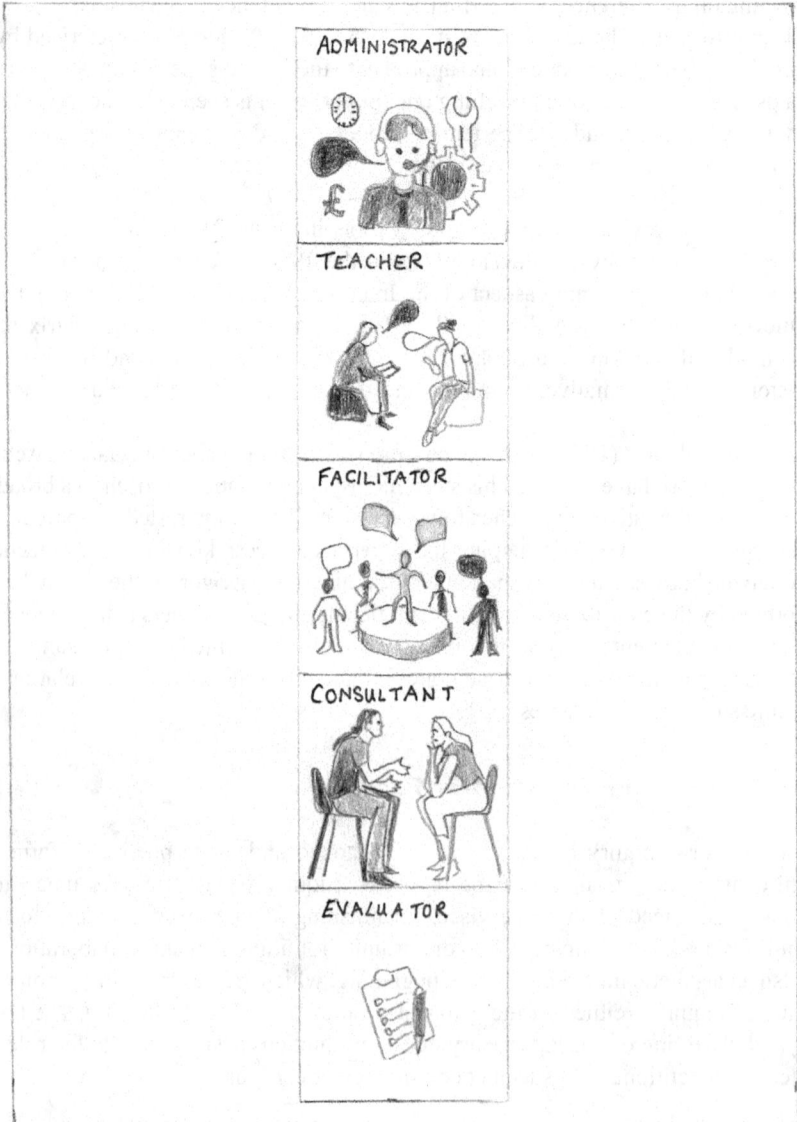

Figure 3.1 Supervisor Roles

The supervisor as Administrator might be seen as the most practical role, dealing with issues of the frame. When the frame is undermined, as we know from therapy and related fields, there is an impact on the work at hand.

Specific tasks related to the supervisor as Administrator are as follows:

- Co-creating a clear contract for the supervisory work and frame
- Ensuring an appropriate space, time and frequency of supervision sessions
- Managing and addressing issues around attendance (frequency and punctuality)
- Managing and addressing issues around payment
- Managing and addressing issues around communication as to the frame.

The supervisor as Teacher takes responsibility for having experience, knowledge and clinical wisdom in some professional area that may be of use to the supervisee. The neophyte supervisor may be challenged by the asymmetry of the roles here.

Specific tasks related to the supervisor as Teacher are as follows:

- Explaining practice, theory and conventions.
- Identifying learning needs.
- Imparting knowledge.
- Modelling technique and facilitating practice of these.
- Encouraging the supervisee to articulate what they know and are less clear about.
- Questioning the supervisee in order to surface areas of confusion or contradiction.
- Setting reading or other learning tasks.
- Setting goals for further sessions offering interpretations or perspectives on the material from the reported work.

The supervisor as Facilitator is closest to the role of practitioner, giving opportunities for the supervisee to explore and discover for themselves.

Specific tasks related to the supervisor as Facilitator are as follows:

- Eliciting a supervisory question, curiosity, concern or need.
- Purposefully guiding or questioning the supervisee to support them towards self-awareness in relation to the work.
- Giving space for the expression of the emotional impact of the supervisee's work.
- Giving opportunities for exploring the supervisee's responses to clients, including identification or repulsion.
- Giving opportunities for exploring the supervisee's responses to the material.
- Giving opportunities for exploring supervisee's responses to the setting.
- Conducting appropriate creative supervision structures and managing the hygiene of these.

The supervisor as Consultant acknowledges the relative parity of the supervisory relationship. The supervisee is recognised for their own clinical experience and wisdom and there is a collaborative approach to reflecting together. The supervisor holds the space and contributes to the dialogue, while the supervisee benefits from a collegial rapport and a space to explore within a clear frame. It is important for the supervisor not to get stuck in this role with the supervisee. It may be the baseline for the relationship, but the other roles and functions may come to the fore from time to time.

Specific tasks related to the supervisor as Consultant are as follows:

- Collaborating with the supervisee to reflect on the issues.
- Exploring options rather than answers.
- Providing a dialogical space to look at wider professional and career development issues.
- Sharing similar experiences related to the supervisory enquiry.
- Intervening at a strategic rather than teaching level.
- Attending to the multiple systems at play.

The supervisor as Evaluator includes the function of judging and assessing. This can be a challenging role for new supervisors, who may have built their practice on the basis of non-judgemental attitudes and are in the early stages of warming up to the implicit authority of the supervisor role. Since the supervisor has a legal and professional duty to monitor safe and ethical practice, this is a necessary and vital role to engage with. The supervisor needs to develop the art of giving feedback in a straightforward and appropriate way and to take responsibility for this aspect of the task of supervision.

Specific tasks related to the supervisor as Evaluator are as follows:

- Following up on interventions and agreed tasks from previous sessions.
- Monitoring and addressing ethical standards and safe practice.
- Giving feedback on areas of strength and weakness relating to theory, technique, professionalism and personal style.
- Confronting when necessary.
- Structuring review sessions and relating these to the supervisory contract.

The Eight Eyes or Modes

These are developed from Hawkins and Shohet. This model helps define the nature of the focus of the enquiry. We define these in the following way:

Eye One: the content, story or bare bones. This might refer to the content of a session or meeting or event; the history of a referral or piece of work; the client's presentation, history and basic information. Eye One also includes the frame, where the work is happening, how it is being funded and who is part of the system.

Eye Two: the strategies and interventions. This eye focuses on 'How to' enquiries at both strategic and skills levels. Interventions refers to the techniques and skills we use as practitioners, while strategies refers more to an overall response to a presenting issue arising in the work.

Eye Three and Four: These belong together as they focus on the dance of the therapeutic or working relationship. They are also distinct, and we find it useful to separate out the emphasis in Eye Three as being the client's or other's experience (including transference or tele from their point of view). Eye Four focuses on the therapist/supervisee's experience (including various kinds of countertransference and tele). Tele is a Morenian term for qualities of relationship that include positive, negative and neutral valences in relationship. It goes beyond the notion of the distortions that are part of transference and countertransference in psychodynamic terms (see Chesner, 2022).

Eye Five: This is the parallel process, particularly understood as how the 'there and then' of the workplace dynamic is unconsciously reproduced in the 'here and now' of the supervision session.

Eye Six: This refers to the countertransference and tele phenomena of the supervisor in the session, particularly unconscious resonances with trauma and the unspoken or unacknowledged phenomena of the direct work being reflected on.

Eye Seven: This relates to the bigger picture, including ecological, political, social, economic and cultural forces that impact people at every level of the system.

We value the Hawkins and Shohet conceptualisation of these Modes or Eyes as belonging to an overlapping double matrix, in which there is an interplay between the direct work system and the supervision system. Within the supervision session the focus may usefully shift between the direct work system and the here and now of the supervision session and both can be conceptualised as part of a bigger picture.

We have somewhat re-articulated the description of these modes or eyes to respond to the requirements of our contemporary creative supervision training. We also propose the addition of an eighth eye.

Eye Eight: This refers to practitioner identity. This eye relates to the practitioner's sense of self in the work. It goes beyond notions of professional performance and efficacy and includes existential and ontological dimensions. It has links with Eye Four, which attends to the practitioner's process, but from a wider perspective than that of the therapeutic or working relationship with the client or in a specific piece of work. It attends to the question, 'Who am I?' and 'How does my professional identity sit within the wider perspective of my life and context?'.

The Integrative Developmental Model (Stoltenberg and McNeill, 2010)

This most researched developmental model tracks professional growth across various domains of competence which can be applied to self as supervisor/supervisor in training and as practitioner or therapist. It is a very detailed framework and subdivides the areas of competency of the practitioner into the following domains: intervention skills competence, assessment techniques, interpersonal assessment, client conceptualisation, individual differences, theoretical orientation, treatment plans and goals and professional ethics. While we do not attend specifically and methodically to each of these domains, we do draw on the three (plus) levels of development as defined in this book. The description of levels is applicable to professional growth and expertise beyond the realm of therapy. Within each of these levels it is worth noting that attention is paid to self- and other awareness (cognitive and affective), motivation and autonomy. The authors refer to their supervisees as trainees, perhaps in line with American norms and reflective of their position as academics educating psychologists. In our European context and experience, supervisees are equally likely to be qualified practitioners as trainees. The description of levels of development is helpful in considering supervisee competencies in both trainee and graduate professionals. In summary, these are the levels:

The Level 1 Therapist

When learning a new modality or working in a new setting, the therapist or practitioner tends to experience anxiety. Supervisees at this level may seek the security of following a given procedure or technique and need assurance as to their competence. They may be confused and unable to think creatively, and at a feeling level they tend to need to focus on themselves and their own performance.

In essence the experience of being a relatively new learner brings with it elements of regression and there is a consequently high level of both anxiety and dependency on the supervisor. The supervisor can usefully structure the supervision sessions and give guidance to the supervisee about conducting and managing their clinical work.

In terms of the five supervisory roles, the supervisor is frequently called on to inhabit teacher and evaluator roles and to model good administrative processes.

The Level 1 Supervisor

A trainee supervisor may also be at Level 1 in their supervision identity. They too may experience performance anxiety, be over focused on how they are doing, and seek to function according to given protocols rather than being in a creative and confident flow. This may lead them to take on a pseudo-expert role with the supervisees, as a defence against their own uncertainties, or to avoid the expert position and some of the helpful authority of the supervisor role. This could include an avoidance of the evaluator role of the supervisor. A Level 1 supervisor may be a good fit with a Level 1 practitioner but is likely to find a

Level 2 practitioner more challenging and is also likely to be a poor fit with a Level 3 practitioner.

The Level 2 Therapist

At this level the therapist is able to focus on the client more as their anxiety about their own competence lessens. This means that the therapist is faced with more complexity, which in turn may bring up anxiety, frustration and confusion. Opening up to the complexity of the client material may be emotionally overwhelming and there is the danger of over-identification with the client. Whilst some aspects of the work are now approached with confidence there may be a resistance to acknowledging a lack of competency in other areas.

The supervisory relationship may be analogous to that of the adolescent and parent in terms of the dependency – autonomy conflict. The supervisor may usefully monitor at which level the supervisee is functioning in each area of their practice and facilitate learning and development to the next level.

In terms of supervisory roles, the supervisor is called upon to role model flexibility, moving from consultant to evaluator and facilitator in response to the changing needs of the supervisee. The role of teacher needs to be used mindfully as the therapist/supervisee will be less keen to be told what to do or how to do it but may be open to a more facilitative teacher/educator style. This is a key phase in the development of the reflexive practitioner.

The Level 2 Supervisor

As trainee or neophyte supervisors move into this level of functioning as a supervisor the complexity of the task of supervision becomes more apparent, and they may experience some of the confusion and conflict about the role of supervisor that parallels that of the Level 2 practitioner. It can be disconcerting to have achieved a level of comfortableness and competence as a practitioner, and to be aware that they are not as confident or competent in the newer role of supervisor. This can lead to an avoidance of some of the supervisory tasks such as the need to make specific evaluations of the supervisee's strengths and learning needs or to embrace the complexity of the role and sustain the effort to grow as a supervisor.

We address this in the training in a number of ways. Firstly, we name the second module of the course as 'Practice Issues' and are explicit about this stage being one of being able to see the complexity of the role. We explore nuances of the role of supervisor together, such as the boundary between supervision and therapy. Level 2 supervisors may be tempted to behave as a counsellor or therapist with supervisees (Stoltenberg and McNeill, 2010: 204) so this is a useful time to engage with perceived grey areas between these two ways of being. We also consider the kind of extra demands that may come to the supervisor beyond simply supervising client or direct work. These demands include the need to write reports, references or evaluations for supervisees and the need to respond to 'crisis' issues and requests that emerge between supervision sessions.

By working together as a group on how to approach such 'crises' we aim to support the supervisor through this phase of learning. We use a number of brief vignettes based on real-life difficulties supervisors have faced and ask the trainees in small groups and within a short time frame to identify (a) what the issues are, (b) what their options might be and (c) what they would choose to do. This three-stage investigation gives the trainee supervisors autonomy but also a supportive structure that they can practise and internalise in preparation for such real-life demands.

We also include as part of this module a peer evaluation task. The rationale for this is to support the trainees to embrace the complexity of maintaining a supportive role with supervisees whilst stepping up to the evaluator role in a clear and balanced way. We wait until the group is bonded and group members have built personal and collegial relationships with each other which mirror the kind of supportive relationship we would hope to have with supervisees. At this point they are asked to do the uncomfortable thing – to give balanced, authentic and owned feedback to their peers. This is a written exercise done quietly and is often perceived as a rite of passage that helps the trainee supervisors move beyond Level 2 functioning as supervisors. Consideration is given to what good feedback is, and there is a long warmup to the moment of this exercise. They are asked to consider their peers' 'ways of being' (i.e. functioning roles) as group members, as supervisors and communicators (e.g. when giving presentations or feedback in practice triads). These reflections are summarised in a short statement about observed strengths, learning needs or areas for development, and any areas of concern.

We hold the space while these written pieces of feedback are read, and in their self-evaluations for this module trainees are invited to summarise what feedback they have received and how they have responded to it. We are explicit about their choices in this – some feedback may be helpful to take on board, and other feedback may be rejected, or understood as being more about their peer than themselves.

The Level 3 Therapist

The Level 3 practitioner or therapist has enough practice to be able to handle the basic skills of running a session without a great deal of conscious rehearsal. They have achieved what Schön defines as knowing in action (KIA) (Schön, 1983: 87). They are able to deal with the relational task of holding a session, link different areas of knowledge, and consider various possible formulations and directions of work. Because these areas of competency are more accessible to the practitioner and to some extent they run as if on automatic, this can allow the therapist to operate a different kind of free-floating attention that is potentially creative in its own right, whether or not creative action methods are part of the practice. Bradford Keeney in The Creative Therapist (2015) describes the meta-level of attention that allows the therapist to notice moments where spontaneity and creativity are possible. He conceptualises this as moving into Act Two of a three-act structure, a moment which opens the door for a client to go beyond the circular recapitulation of a problem into something that reframes it and allows for a new perspective. This process is completely compatible with Moreno's Cycle of Spontaneity and Creativity (Moreno in Fox, 1987) whereby the initial problem or narrative is repeated as a cultural conserve, and the therapist seeks the moment of potential spontaneity that can lead to a creative reframing.

The supervisor working with a supervisee operating largely at this level will be in a more consultative role relationship. The supervisee tends to be more able to identify their supervisory concerns, and there is a less hierarchical dimension to the sessions. The supervisor can draw on their own experience whilst acknowledging that the supervisee has more experience or competence in some areas of the work being explored.

The Level 3 Supervisor

Supervisors who continue to grow and reflect can move beyond their Level 2 functioning to a place of integration, stable motivation and a good level of mastery of the art and craft of supervision. Supervision of supervision is an invaluable resource for this continued growth. In the UK most psychotherapy and counselling bodies encourage or insist on some level of supervision specific continued professional development (CPD) and supervision of supervision practice.

In our own training we note that most cohorts create one or more peer groups at the end of their training, through which they give each other ongoing peer supervision of supervision and keep the collegial valuing of creative supervision alive. This does not preclude specific one-to-one supervision of supervision but is highly valued as supporting a sense of community amongst creative supervisors.

In conclusion, this chapter briefly recapitulates the historical background of supervision and where we see creative supervision sitting within this. We articulate our emphasis in creative supervision on focusing the supervision enquiry through a supervisory question or focus. We revisit the bodies of theory that inform our theoretical approach to supervision, summarising their key points and our adaptations to these, in particular the fifth role of the supervisor and the articulation of an eighth eye or mode. We touch on the interplay between the theory of supervisor roles and the IDM levels of both supervisor and supervisee.

References

Basa, V., 2017. "Models of Supervision in Therapy, Brief Defining Features". *European Journal of Counselling Theory, Research and Practice, 1, 4*, 1–5.

Chesner, A., 2022. *Tele, Transference and Countertransference in Supervision* in *Zeitschrift Psychodrama Soziometrie*. Springer.

Hawkins, P., and Shohet, R., 2012. *Supervision in the Helping Professions* (4th edition). Open University Press.

Inskipp, F., and Proctor, B., 1993. *The Art, Craft and Tasks of Counselling Supervision*. Cascade Publications.

Keeney, B., 2015. *The Creative Therapist*. Routledge.
Moreno, J.L., 1940, in Fox, J. ed., 1987. *The Essential Moreno*. Springer.
Schön, D.A., 1983. *The Reflective Practitioner*. Basic Books.
Stoltenberg, C.D., and McNeill, B.W., 2010. *IDM Supervision, an Integrative Developmental Model for Supervising Counselors and therapists*. Routledge.
Williams, A., 1995. *Visual and Active Supervision*. Norton.

Part II

Creative Techniques as Applied to Supervision

Chapter 4

Small World Technique

Anna Chesner

Figure 4.0

In Chapter 2 on Warmup, we introduced the use of objects to represent expectations of the supervisor and supervisee towards each other. We named these as props, using a term taken from theatre. The psychodramatic term for the use of concrete objects onto which meaning is projected or in which meaning is held is 'concretisation'. Concretisation is a projective technique, and one which is particularly useful in supervision and reflective practice. It allows the creator to view a system from the outside, from above and at some aesthetic distance. Considering the Latin derivation of the word supervision this is perhaps the technique most suited to the practice of supervision (from the Latin *super* for above or over and the Latin *videre* for seeing).

The same principle, of concretisation, is used in the supervisory technique of 'Small World'. In this case the scale of the image made by the supervisee is reduced, accentuating the contrast between the perspective of the viewer and the made image. It gives the supervisee a bird's eye view.

DOI: 10.4324/9781003435655-7

Requirements

Plain cloth or paper is required to provide the background – a designation of what is onstage and what is offstage.

Small objects such as buttons, stones, shells, small ornaments and items from doll's houses are required. Collections can be restricted to objects from the natural world, such as stones, shells, twigs and leaves, in which case a variety of textures, shape and colour would be important. It can be helpful to add to these animal figurines, mythical characters in miniature, coins, keys and pieces of ribbon or string.

An optional piece of equipment for small world is the Communicube or Communiwell that was developed by John Casson, drawing on his training in dramatherapy and psychodrama. These five-tiered transparent structures, the size of a small coffee table, take the place of the cloth or paper used to create the stage for the small world. Their added value is the possibility of depicting relationships in layers or levels.

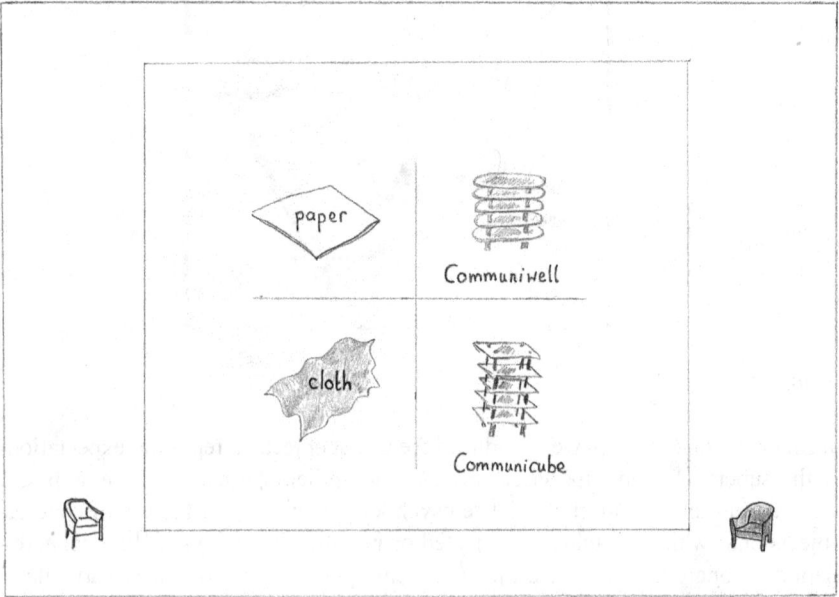

Figure 4.1 Action Area for Small World

Step-by-Step Guide to Facilitating Small World within a Supervision Session

Firstly, identify a supervisory question or concern. This initial process is crucial in terms of ensuring an appropriate focus for the creative work within supervision.

Working creatively has its own momentum and can seem meaningful and reward-ing because of how engaging it is. However, much may be missed if the specific supervisory need is not identified. Some supervisees will arrive at a session with one or more prepared supervisory questions. Others may need a general discus-sion about their work and more collaborative support in teasing out an appropriate supervisory need or outcome to the session. As practitioners our ability to be spe-cific about our learning edge and our sense of something unresolved or disturbing in our work grows with experience, especially if regular supervision encourages our curiosity and the articulation of a supervisory question or focus.

Here are some sample supervisory questions from different settings:

a My client has made a number of important changes in therapy. Do I still have something to offer, or should we be moving towards closure?
b In team meetings one of my direct reports isn't finding their voice. I don't know what to make of it and whether it is my responsibility to draw her out. What are my options?
c My therapy group is never complete. It has been weeks since we were all pre-sent. I don't know what to do about it or what is going on.

Secondly, before going into a deeper discussion or an action exploration of the issue it is worth taking a moment to do some *backstage thinking* (Chesner, 2024). Depending on the supervisory relationship this might be articulated out loud or it may be better held as an internal guide as to what to include and emphasise in the facilitation of the action technique. Backstage thinking links theoretical super-visory considerations to the particular supervisory enquiry.

Taking the supervisory questions above as examples. Question (a) appears to be an Eye Two enquiry, relating to strategies and interventions, whether to sug-gest moving towards closure, perhaps to recontract about the current focus of the therapy work, or maybe to say nothing and wait for the client to bring up the sub-ject of potential closure. There might be Eye Three and Four dimensions to the question in terms of a changing therapeutic relationship as the work has progressed or an Eye Seven factor in terms of an internal or external pressure to close the work in favour of taking on new clients.

Question (b) relates to a non-therapy third-sector setting. The enquiry has some-thing to do with role clarity for the supervisee – what belongs within their own area of responsibility and how interventionist to be with the perceived developmental needs of their team members. As such the focus could be seen as an Eye One ques-tion, looking at how the team meetings function currently and what happens and doesn't happen in them. It also relates to Eye Seven factors – the culture of the organisation, the motivation and role requirements of team members, the dynamics within the team and the job description of the supervisee and the different team members.

Question (c) is an Eye Three and Eye Four enquiry, relating to what might be going on between the group members of the therapy group, including the therapist. It may well include factors of transference and countertransference. At another level it is an Eye One question, how the recent history of the group may be affecting attendance, and an Eye Two question, how to reset the culture of the therapy group and how to address issues of absence and presence.

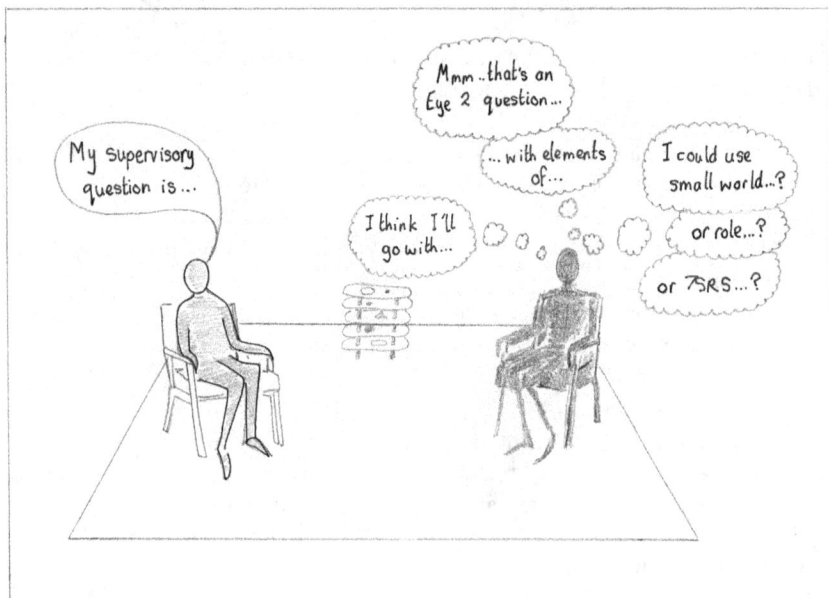

Figure 4.2 Backstage Thinking

In addition to these reflections on the eight eyes or modes in supervision (see Chapter 3) the supervisor may also remind themselves at this point of the IDM levels of the supervisees – are they at a level where they will welcome a teaching or guiding input, or are they more in a place of needing the supervisor as consultant, holding the space for autonomous, facilitated self-reflection?

The moment of backstage thinking that occurs between identifying the supervisory question and offering a creative facilitation serves as a brief orientation for the supervisor as they choose whether to offer an action-oriented exploration, and in their consideration of which one may be of most benefit.

Facilitation of the Method Step by Step

1 Choose a cloth/sheet of paper as background or stage for this exploration. You, the supervisee, determine the size, colour and texture. Lay it out on the floor or table surface.

2 Explore the small objects that are available, whether in a container or on the shelves of the consulting room.

3 Begin by choosing one or more objects to represent yourself and an object to represent the significant others in this situation.

For example, in question (a) this may refer simply to the therapist and the client; in question (b) it may refer to the team leader, the direct report who is seen as withholding or quiet, and the other team members; in question (c) it may refer to the therapist, the group members who are present and those who are absent.

4 Place the objects in relation to each other in a way that makes sense to you or feels right. Consider both proxemics and the direction in which they are facing and their relationship with each other.

5 Choose objects to add any other factors or people that feel relevant to your enquiry.

For example in question (a) this might include the themes of the work that have already been addressed, and those that have not been. In question (b) there may be something for the line management expectations of the supervisee, something of the culture or the pressure of the organisation as a whole, maybe something historic, such as team members who are no longer present, but whose story haunts the team dynamic, and maybe something to represent the personal or systemic factors that might be inhibiting the contribution of the quiet team member. In question (c) it may be relevant to add lines of tension and unresolved issues between team members or thoughts and fantasies in the mind of the therapist when with the group. If the therapist is a trainee, then the training school's expectations about attendance may also usefully be concretised.

6 Contemplate the image created.

Note: The small world image that exists in the third space between supervisor and supervisee gives a visual focus for discussion. It brings the 'there and then' into the 'here and now' of the reflective space, for both to contemplate together. The supervisor can ask what the supervisee sees, whether it is accurate, whether something is missing, and how they feel about what they notice. This may be enough, particularly if the supervisory question is held in mind as a lens through which to view the small world sculpt.

7 Additional options when using small world:

- Use a piece of ribbon, string or peg to show where the alliances, tensions and boundaries are.
- Trace with your finger where there is a smooth dynamic and where there is tension, using a zigzag movement for tension and a smooth movement for an easeful dynamic.
- How would you like it to look? Show me. What would need to change in order for that to happen? Either return it to how it is in reality or keep the image of desired change.
- Place your finger on an object representing one of the other people or roles within the system and speak from that role.

Note: A note about this last optional intervention. This is a version of role-taking or role-reversing adapted to the small world frame. As we will see in the next chapter, role-taking and interviewing in role can be a profound experience through which the supervisee steps into the shoes of the other, changes perspective temporarily, and has access to a double or multiple description of the situation presented. While classical psychodramatic role reversal is an embodied experience, beginning with a change of position and posture there is always an element of empathic imagination involved. When working with small world the primary means of engagement is projective and imaginative. The physicality of placing the finger on the object representing the other is minimal compared to a full embodied role reversal, but the power of empathic imagination means that even this gesture can facilitate a profound shift in perception. When interviewing in role it is advisable for the supervisor to adapt the questions they pose to the supervisee-in-role to the supervisory question or focus agreed upon. For example, in question (a) the supervisee may be asked to place their finger on the object representing their client and the supervisor could ask "How long have you been in therapy? I understand you have achieved quite a lot. What have been the biggest changes for you? If I were to say to you that your therapist is wondering if it is time to move towards an ending, how does that land with you?" In question (b) rather than immediately interviewing the silent team member in role it might be helpful to get the perspective of a different team member, perhaps with the following questions: "How long have you been in this team? Who does most of the talking? Whose ideas do you value? How do you experience your colleague here, who is quiet? Is it only in team meetings that they are quiet? What do you make of that? And your manager, what do you notice with her?" The questions are still geared to the enquiry about the dynamic and impact of the silent team member, but the perspective is broadened, and the supervisee gets to look at the situation, including their own role in it, through the eyes of another. In question (c) it might be helpful to do a brief interview-in-role with each group member, those present and those absent from the therapy group and to build up an awareness of the multiple perspectives on the complex dynamic of a therapy group. There can be an element of circular questioning about their perception of the group dynamic, other group members, their own reasons for not attending, as well as their fantasy about others' absences. The important thing is to include the primary focus of attendance and non-attendance, but to warm up the supervisee briefly into the role of each group member before addressing the hot question.

Through all these interventions the supervisee gets the opportunity to hold an overview of the situation being explored, whilst also being in touch with the different subjective perspectives within it. The supervisor can invite the supervisee-in-the-supervision-room to speak to the small world image of self in the work environment. These might be words of encouragement, advice or challenge.

If the supervisor gets the sense that the small world focus is becoming rigid or too intense another useful intervention is to invite the supervisee to stand, move around the space and view the small world from different perspectives, reflecting on what they now notice.

8 Derole the image and move into a final discussion. Supervisor or supervisee may take a photo of the small world image as a record before deroling it. Deroling means releasing the objects from the projected meaning of the small world sculpt and clearing them away, as well as the background cloth or paper. We use the term deroling rather than clearing away as a reminder of the projective nature of the method. There is a symmetry to the structure of the session, in that we begin in dialogue, without creative action methods, and we finish in dialogue, with any third space constructions having been deroled.

9 This frees up the attention for a purely here-and-now dialogue. This is an opportunity to revisit the supervisory question and to reflect on how it has been addressed and any action points to take away. Characteristically this phase of the work is less intense and part of the process of either closing the session or moving on to a new focus where the timing of the work allows for this.

Small World Technique in Group Supervision

There are a number of options for using small world within a supervision group setting. See Chapter 7 for ways of working with groups. If there is agreement to focus on one person's presentation the group witnesses the creation of the small world image and may be invited to ask questions about what they see once it has been set up. There may be a time-limited free-floating reflective space before the supervisor moves the process towards closure and deroling. The time allocated for dialogue after the deroling of the image should be long enough for all group members to reflect on the significance of the work for them, naming any points of resonance and learning.

The method can also be used by multiple group members working individually at the start of a session to briefly show a situation that is on their mind, introduce it to the group and share their supervisory question. Depending on the group size and length of the session there can either be a group choice as to whose sculpt to focus on, in which case the other sculpts get deroled at this point, or time is allocated to attend to each person's enquiry in turn. It is the supervisor's task to make sure that each enquiry is appropriately time-boundaried.

A third possibility which is particularly suited to teams, where the client or situation being explored is known to all members is the creation of a collaborative small world. Team members negotiate which object to use to represent who or what from the supervisory question and the proxemics and spatial relationship of the objects. In this activity much of the reflective work is done during the collaborative creation of the small world sculpt.

Small World Technique in Online Supervision

When working with small world online we are reliant on our supervisees having the necessary collection of small world objects and cloth or paper to hand. This can be done by planning ahead or contracting for various materials to be at hand during online supervision sessions, whether for small world or other creative techniques. Suitably sized objects can be found in the kitchen, bathroom, desktop or outdoors. A collection of 20–30 objects is plenty.

Something to bear in mind is that the supervisee will continue to be around these objects after the session, so it may be worth clarifying whether more personal objects, such as jewellery or make-up, are appropriate to use for the work. This is a matter of sensitivity. I have known enthusiastic jewellery wearers to be quite comfortable taking their rings off their hands to represent quite challenging roles in a small world sculpt and afterwards putting them back on without any sense of or concern about psychological contamination. For others it may be better to have a small bag or box of items that will be used specifically for work purposes and that can be put away afterwards.

Ideally the supervisor has sight both of the small world as it is being made, and of the supervisee in the making of it as we would in an in-person session. A laptop can be easily angled in either direction – onto the face of the supervisee or tilted to take in a tabletop small world sculpt. Where a heavier or more rigid computer is being used the supervisor can guide the supervisee to set up a second device, such as a mobile phone on a stand, which can be visible, without audio, angled to take in the small world stage. That way the supervisor can take in both the supervisee and the small world. This solution takes some preparation and will be easier for more technologically fluent supervisees. Once the supervisory pair has worked out the mechanics of doing this technique online it will be easier on future occasions.

The same process as for in-person supervision is used in facilitating the piece of work.

Working with the Communicube or Communiwell

The Communicube and Communiwell function as a theatrical stage for small world work. The same principles apply to the facilitation of the method as have been described above. The added dimension is the spatial relationship between the five transparent layers. The layers can be used to depict different time perspectives, or different psychological layers, or different contextual influences on the supervisory issue explored.

Let us consider the first supervisory question above:

My client has made a number of important changes in therapy. Do I still have something to offer, or should we be moving towards closure?

Here it could be helpful to depict the here-and-now state of the therapeutic relationship on the top layer. Each layer beneath could be used to symbolise phases of the relationship, or topics that have been addressed and worked through. One or more layers might be used to create an image of the material that has not been addressed or not worked through.

Seeing these multiple images at the same time opens up an arena for dialogue between supervisee and supervisor about the question of potential closure. In a very succinct way, the imagery created on the Communicube or Communiwell encapsulates the story of the therapy relationship, as well as an overview of change and potential change.

Because there is always to some degree an unconscious communication when working with projective techniques there might be surprises and new insights that might not be so apparent if the supervisory question were approached purely verbally.

Taking the second supervisory question above:

In team meetings one of my direct reports isn't finding their voice. I don't know what to make of it and whether it is my responsibility to draw her out. What are my options?

In this case the top layer might be used to represent the dynamics in team meetings, and the supervisee might add other contextual factors that could be relevant on the lower layers. These factors might include historical moments within the team or organisation that might be contributing to the direct report communicating less. They might also depict what the supervisee knows about the personal history or circumstances of the direct report in question. Again, just marking out these hidden or deeper perspectives informs the dialogue around the supervisory question.

In the case of the third supervisory question above:

My therapy group is never complete. It has been weeks since we were all present. I don't know what to do about it or what is going on.

Here the top level might represent the sense of the group dynamic as it is – perhaps marking who is more central, who is closer to whom, etc.

The other levels can be used to focus either on individuals in the group and the supervisee's sense of their inner world, or possibly particular dyads or subgroups, or themes which are being addressed and not addressed within the group. Any of these approaches could be a useful intervention. My own approach is to be transparent about my sense of the possible ways of using the layers and ask the supervisee which of these feels most helpful or indeed whether they have another idea.

An example of the power and efficacy of this method is described here by Lewis Pickles, a trainee dramatherapist.

"During the final phase of my training as a dramatherapist, I engaged with the Communicube in a supervision session. It is a creative tool that supported me to capture the complexity of my placement experiences. As a trainee, I found that the method provided a tangible, visual structure through which

I could externalise and explore the intricate web of relationships within my clinical work. By projecting aspects of my practice into objects and placing them in relation to one another, I was able to view my client work as part of a broader systemic constellation.

I began the process by selecting a small object to represent myself, a glass bottle, which I placed on the second-lowest layer of the cube. This object reflected my inner container. It was fuelling my practice and open to receiving the experiences that arose in therapy. Around it, I arranged some objects to symbolise the clients I had worked with across different placements. One by one, the figures formed a network of relationships that echoed not only the clinical dynamics but also my own internal responses to the work. This sculptural approach allowed me to witness how the threads of different client experiences intersected, diverged, or merged within my therapeutic practice.

Among these, one object stood out, a large dragonfly, which I placed on the bottom layer. This figure came to represent the intensity of my placement in an acute psychiatric setting, where I experienced strong somatic counter-transference. The dragonfly's expansive presence on the lowest layer visually embodied how deeply that work resonated with my own unconscious material. It symbolised the emotional and embodied impact of that placement, which I came to understand as a foundational influence running beneath all my other clinical experiences. Another key moment arose when I placed a small wooden heart with a hole in it on the top layer of the cube, representing a client whose presence had lingered with me. At first, the object's distance from the 'self' bottle felt disconnected. However, as I shifted slightly in my seat, I noticed that the hole in the heart aligned directly with the glass bottle, creating a visual line of connection. This simple shift brought a realisation: despite apparent distance, there was a vital and meaningful connection between this client and a central part of myself, perhaps even the part that fuels my therapeutic work. The visual metaphor enabled me to access a new layer of insight into our relationship. What I found most useful with the Communicube was its capacity to reveal the unseen. Through this ephemeral sculptural method, the layers of my experience were externalised and made visible. The cube offered a dynamic structure that mirrored the evolving nature of my development as a dramatherapist. It became a container in which all aspects of my practice (my clients, myself, and the relational fields between us) could co-exist. In this way, the Communicube became a creative mirror of my inner world and professional journey. As a learning tool, it allowed for a deeper witnessing of the therapeutic process, one that moved beyond verbal reflection into the embodied and symbolic. For me, it was a supportive medium through which I could explore and integrate different placement experiences within supervision".

Reference

Chesner A., 2024. "Backstage Thinking in One to One Psychodrama Psychotherapy". *Zeitschrift für Psychodrama und Soziometrie*, 23(1), 27–37. https://doi.org/10.1007/s11620-024-00826-z

Chapter 5

Working with the Psychodramatic Techniques of Role, Double and Mirror

Anna Chesner

Figure 5.0

In this chapter I am addressing both 'role theory' and the techniques of 'working with role', the 'psychodramatic double' and 'mirror'. Understanding role theory supports the supervision process in many ways, regardless of whether the technique of working with role is applied in a session. It is helpful in refining a supervisory question or focus as well as making sense of what is communicated through the various other creative supervision techniques described in this book.

DOI: 10.4324/9781003435655-8

For this reason, the chapter begins with a summary of role theory as applied to supervision and moves on to the use of role work, doubling and mirroring as techniques within individual and group supervision. I base this chapter on my previous publication (Chesner and Zografou 2014, Chapter 3) which I have revised and expanded.

Definition of Role[1]

Role is a way of being. As such we embody roles throughout our lives. According to Moreno, role is the functioning form the individual takes in any moment (Moreno, 1987a: 62). It is not limited as a concept to the idea of donning a mask or a persona. In common parlance 'playing a role' is an expression that might be used to denote falseness or inauthenticity. We might think of Edgar in King Lear or Iago in Othello, characters for whom there is a chilling gulf between their presentation to the world and their inner motivation. They play a role, in order to deceive. They operate in the realm of seeming rather than being. In psychodramatic thinking, by contrast, being appropriate to the moment, embodying spontaneity, is dependent on having a wide and flexible enough role repertoire to 'be' authentic. This value is clearly an important one when considering clinical or professional practice. As therapists, coaches and other practitioners we need the capacity to be congruent, to embody a good level of authenticity. This is the foundation for a healthy supervision culture, one in which our supervisees can open up to themselves and achieve authenticity and spontaneity in their own practice and encourage these qualities in their clients. In this sense a wide role repertoire supports the encounter.

Three Categories of Role

Moreno distinguishes three broad categories of role: somatic, social and psychodramatic. They relate to his theory of child development and the development of the self, and each has a relevance to supervision practice.

Somatic Roles

From before birth we are embodied organisms and from birth we breathe, move, digest and sleep. An infant will often be described in terms of how it engages with these functions, such as a good feeder and an erratic sleeper. As we mature these somatic roles continue to have a profound effect on us both intrapsychically and socially. As van der Kolk (2015) writes the body does indeed keep the score. Attention to the body and the body–mind system underpins current wisdom on trauma work. The field of mindfulness as a psychological tool depends on somatic awareness, of the breath, posture, gestures and senses. By attending to these we can learn to self-soothe, self-reflect and be present.

Social Roles

This category of role is also present from before birth. The growing baby exists in relation to the mother, and the mother-to-be warms up to and grows into the role of mother over time. This dependence on and interdependence with others continues until death. Social roles define our relationships, whether with the family (brother, sister, daughter, uncle), within the workplace (chief executive, personal assistant, cleaner, actor, teacher) and in our social life (spouse, lover, resident, migrant, group member).

In Morenian terms it is not enough just to name the somatic or social role. It is the *way* that we engage with that role that is key. A 'shallow breather', an 'enthusiastic runner', an 'exhausted, resentful mother' and a 'bored lover' – these roles with a descriptor give concise thumbnail sketches of ways of being and offer useful ways of describing aspects of ourselves and our clients in practice.

Psychodramatic Roles

The third category of role takes us into the dimension of metaphor and imagination. These are psychological or psychodramatic roles. They exist in the world of fantasy and imagination. Whilst existing primarily in the internal world of the individual this inner world can inspire and influence external lived reality. Some psychodramatic roles may function as role models. As an example from my own life I remember being in a workshop run by Jonathan Fox some years ago, and he had a gentle and subtle way of letting us know when it was time to leave our small group discussions and come back to the group as a whole. He played a flute, the sounds of which gradually penetrated our awareness, without rudely interrupting or cutting off our process in a sudden way. Since then, when needing to call back small group discussions I channel my inner Jonathan and sing as a way of getting the group's attention or vocalise quite gently and repeatedly until the message lands. Following his role model, I am aware that it is unrealistic for people to stop their conversations immediately whilst knowing that singing or calling will eventually land and achieve the desired result.

How many of us sing in the shower, not only to ourselves, but to an imaginary audience of thousands? Or perhaps we confront or punish someone who has hurt us in the privacy of the theatre of our own mind, responding in a way we had no access to at the time? These are conversations which may not be intended to reach the light of day or social reality, but which, with the power of imagination, bring us some sense of completion or re-balancing.

It can be useful to consider what kind of psychodramatic roles inform our clients', colleagues' and our own way of being as practitioners and therapists.

We might express these perceptions through archetypes – for example, a therapist as 'benevolent mother' or as 'playful sparring partner' or through metaphor – for example, a client as 'illusive fish' or as 'hungry baby bird'.

Presenting Client Material Through Role Theory

How do we present our clients to the supervisor, coach or supervision group for reflection? Thinking about somatic roles, we can consider how the client presents physically, their posture, dress and way of moving and whether their presenting issues include a somatic component. We can also notice our own somatic counter-transference response to being with them. Thinking about social roles, we can give an outline of their family situation, their intimate and social relationships and their relationship history. In a coaching context we can share something of their place within different groupings of people, their way of being when performing different functions. The absent roles can be as informative as the present ones. By acknowledging the well-developed functioning roles, we can hold in mind their ego strengths, skills and factors supportive to the work. We can also attend to underdeveloped roles, which may link to therapeutic or coaching goals and needs. Overdeveloped roles and role relationships usually highlight presenting problems or defences. Since roles tend to be reciprocal, eliciting a response or counter-role in the other, we are likely to notice our own role response to different clients and colleagues in a way that can be helpful to reflect on.

Psychodramatic roles are more likely to emerge as the therapeutic work develops, although occasionally we may infer psychodramatic roles quite early on from the way the client describes themselves or others. These roles also come to light through dream material, which presents the inner world through metaphor. It is also useful to consider the psychodramatic roles of an organisation. These are the implicit fantasy roles that exist at a collective level for an organisation and the shadow of these roles. There may or may not be congruence between the overt vision or mission of an organisation and its psychodramatic roles. A service may overtly be dedicated to the care of clients but covertly engaged in a Julius Caesar like power struggle at executive level.

Exercise for the Reader

Make a list of five somatic roles. Thinking about your own ways of being, add a descriptor to each of these (e.g. enthusiastic exerciser, voracious eater, light sleeper).

Make a list of three social roles you have within the family, and again add a descriptor (e.g. resentful sibling, worried son, playful auntie).

Make a list of three social roles related to your work identity, and again add a descriptor (e.g. reluctant manager, diligent responder to emails, confused new team member).

Make a list of a final three social roles that have to do with your friendships, intimate relationships and hobbies, and again add a descriptor (e.g. argumentative partner, enthusiastic calligrapher, reliable confidante).

Consider your psychodramatic roles – identify someone you admire or are fascinated by from history, literature, theatre or film or public life. Write down their name and three words to describe them (e.g. David Attenborough: modest, dedicated to his field, influential). Now try on the same descriptors in relation to yourself. Reflect on how they fit, as a description of how you are or how you would like to be. (e.g. I am Anna and I am modest, dedicated to my field and influential.)

Finally, think about a client and use the same exercise to note what you know or surmise about the client and their somatic, social and psychodramatic roles.

The Use of Role Theory in Reflective Practice

We can use the notions of role repertoire, role clusters and role analysis to understand and initiate change within supervision and coaching.

Role Repertoire

Habit tends to lead to cultural conserves and a limited repertoire of ways of being. It is a sign of increased spontaneity and creativity to have a wider role repertoire. In psychodramatic theory roles can be overdeveloped, underdeveloped or adequate. The COVID-19 pandemic presented us all quite suddenly with challenges to expand our role repertoire. In the world of therapy there were some who decided not to practice online because the unfamiliarity and the loss of the normal frame for the work felt unworkable or unsafe. Others found ways of adapting their practice to online platforms and even developed new ways of being both safe and creative. Online practice has now, some years later, become a norm for some practitioners and a negotiable option for others. Similarly in the world of organisations there is an ongoing balancing of online and office-based work. We have had to learn to be agile, in terms of frames of practice and ways of working. Such agility relates to the idea of role repertoire.

Example 1   Expanding the Role Repertoire

Brenda is a trainee supervisor. She is an experienced creative therapist who creates good working alliances with her therapy clients and enjoys the confidence she has earned as a good facilitator of her creative modality. As she begins her supervision practice, however, she finds it hard to step into the supervisory roles of teacher, consultant or evaluator. Through discussion of her role repertoire as a therapist and as a neophyte supervisor in supervision of supervision she is able to identify and articulate that she is reluctant to take initiative in these new roles. In the world of her psychological or psychodramatic roles the 'holder of authority' is linked with associations of abuse of power. Naturally averse to becoming 'an abusive holder of authority' she finds herself avoiding the authority-based aspects of the new role of supervisor. This limits her capacity to fulfil the evaluative, teacher or consultancy-based aspects of her task with her supervisees, and she approaches the supervision sessions with the same gentle and permissive approach as she uses as a therapist. This narrows her role repertoire and limits her effectiveness and her confidence as a supervisor. In the supervision of supervision session, she is invited to consider non-abusive ways of stepping into authority, to reflect on role models she can identify to help her with this expansion of her role repertoire. Over time she befriends the role of 'appropriate holder of authority' and steps into new ways of being with her supervisees.

Role Clusters

Dalmiro Bustos uses the Morenian notion of role clusters and has developed it from a psychoanalytic perspective (Bustos, 1994). While there are apparently innumerable permutations of role relationships, Moreno noticed that they can be clustered together according to recognisable common dynamics. The concept of maternal, paternal and sibling role clusters is particularly useful in supervision when we are considering relationship or therapeutic style and therapeutic alliance, as well as supervisory style and supervisory relationship. According to the developmental and therapeutic needs of the client at any moment the therapist might usefully model their way of relating according to the holding function of the mother (maternal role cluster), the boundary setting function of the father (paternal role cluster), or they might position themselves more alongside the client (sibling role cluster). Note that the psychoanalytic or archetypal language of maternal or paternal ways of being is not limited by gender. We all have the potential to hold and nurture, set boundaries or be alongside. Our habit may have led us to tend towards one of these more than others.

Example 2   Working with Role Clusters

Supervisee Sarah is struggling with the dynamics of a psychotherapy group she runs. Unlike her one-to-one practice, in which she tends to have strong working alliances with her vulnerable and complex clients, she now finds herself facilitating a deeply resistant group and is the object of overt and covert attacks, which threaten to undermine the culture of the group and are personally difficult to bear. As she explores her role relationships in supervision, it emerges that her way of approaching the therapeutic relationship in each setting is a factor. With most of her one-to-one clients she operates from the maternal role cluster, holding her clients in an empathic way that facilitates deep attachments and a strong working alliance with the dyadic relationship at the centre of the work. She is most comfortable when there is a positive maternal transference and countertransference. In the group setting she tries to position herself in the same way, but the group perceives this as intrusive, creating envy and resentment. All conflict is directed towards her, and she finds herself both overwhelmed and unable to move away from being at the centre of the group, where she has unwittingly placed herself. In supervision she is able to explore her own interventions and ways of being in the group and to identify these as belonging to the maternal role cluster. She engages with the possibility of stepping into a more paternal role cluster, although this is an unfamiliar way of being. It involves her practising not responding immediately and making occasional interventions at a group level rather than to individuals in the group. She finds herself taking a more back-seat position in the group, holding her own boundaries differently and being more dispassionate and firmer in her response to the group dynamics. The group members respond by engaging more with each other, and the group culture shifts into a more productive phase. As a by-product of her expanding her role repertoire in this way she finds herself more able to engage with this role cluster in some of her one-to-one work as well with good effect.

Role Analysis

Role analysis is a specifically psychodramatic way of formulating ways of being that underpins the LCP approach to psychodrama as a psychotherapy and as a way of reflecting on interpersonal and group dynamics. It is particularly useful in going beyond the content or story of a situation and allowing underlying patterns to be revealed and named.

There are five factors of role analysis, which can be understood as a lens, through which we can contemplate a dynamic. These are as follows:

Context: what the *other* is doing, to which there is a role response, for example, when faced with a critical comment from someone in authority or when faced with a plea for sympathy.

Behaviour: the doing component of the role response, including things we do internally and things we refrain from doing, for example, shrinking internally, going quiet, or pushing back.

Feelings: these are the emotional and affective responses to the specific context.

Beliefs: the underlying assumptive way of viewing self, other and the world. These can be deduced collaboratively from exploring context, behaviour and feelings. For example, "I always get things wrong and will never be good enough", "Others know better/are there to support me/ are out to humiliate me", "The world operates on the basis of attack or be attacked."

Consequences: these are the outcomes of the way of being and understanding the world described above. These can be positive or negative. In supervision they often underpin the supervisory question. For example, "Why do I find myself feeling like the outsider in my team, again?"

Example 3   Working with Role Analysis

Patrick, a verbal psychotherapist in private practice, feels overwhelmed by the sheer weight of material presented by his client, Celia. She talks freely in the sessions about a number of different issues and events in her life, often hopping from one apparent narrative to another, from issues with her boyfriend to an ongoing battle with her mother, to concerns she has at work, to friction with a girlfriend, to responses to films she has seen. Patrick wonders what he is doing, where he is going with the work and whether he has anything to offer to the process. He feels like a witness rather than an active participant in the session. In supervision the various narratives of the client are explored, and the following formulation for the client is created, using the five factors of role analysis, that underpins several of the stories she tells.

1 Context: in situations where the other is perceived as putting her under pressure to engage or perform.
2 Behaviour: she digs her heels in, talks fast, resists engaging with the challenge, makes counter-challenges and shifts the pressure onto the other.
3 Feelings: she feels under pressure, anxious and angry.
4 Beliefs: she believes herself to be inadequate to the challenge that she is in danger of disappearing in the relationship, that people are driven by a need to dominate and subjugate and that there is no such thing as give and take.
5 Consequence: she ends up in relationships of unresolved conflict, where there is a stalemate and a lack of intimacy and spontaneity.

By framing what he has learnt about the client in this way, Patrick gains a sense of agency in his thinking about the therapy work. He is able to recognise the dynamic between himself and the client as another example of the pattern she describes in her multiple narratives, and he gets in contact with his productive curiosity as a therapist. Now that he is able to see beneath the overwhelming content of the multiple narratives, he decides to keep an ear open for how she came to develop these beliefs and assumptions about herself, others and the way the world is. He is also able to contextualise his own countertransference responses in the light of the role analysis he has created for the client. He is the 'other' for her, the context she responds to in a habitual way.

Moving into Action – Using Psychodramatic Techniques within Supervision

While the full use of psychodrama methods requires an extensive training of a minimum of four years, we have found that there are discrete applications of role, doubling and mirror that can be taught within the supervision training and applied in service of a supervisory enquiry.

The Psychodramatic Technique of Role in One-to-One Supervision

The first of these is the use of Role, in particular interview-in-role. As a technique it facilitates the therapist/supervisee to get under the skin or into the shoes of a client. It helps to amplify their attention on what the client is communicating and what might be being missed in the therapy or coaching relationship. It is particularly useful when the therapist is too distanced from the client, and it helps to highlight the countertransference and resonances in the practitioner and to increase empathy. Note that it is *not* recommended where the therapist is over-identified with the client or where the material is too overwhelming or disturbing.

I have broken the process down into distinct phases.

Firstly, the supervisor and supervisee agree on a supervisory question or enquiry.

The kind of questions that would indicate use of role as a suitable technique are eye two, three and four questions such as:

Should I suggest working towards an ending? (Eye Two)
What is going on between myself and the client? (Eye Three and Eye Four)
*I wonder how my client sees me in the work and whether they are getting what they
     need (Eye Three)*

Why do I often end up feeling anxious at the end of a session with this client? (Eye Four)

These are all enquiries which would benefit from a sense of the perspective of the other, the client.

Invitation to Action

The supervisee is invited to explore the question through role work.

If they consent, they begin by positioning an empty chair in the space in such a way that its distance and direction fits, communicating something of the felt sense in the relationship.

This task, simple though it is, activates the supervisee's imagination and their sense of the 'as if'. It is 'as if' the client was being brought into the supervisory space. The chair is imaginatively activated or enrolled by the supervisee moving it into position. This will be the space where the action takes place.

The supervisor explains that in a moment the supervisee will move across into that chair and find the posture and way of sitting of the client. Once there the supervisor will talk to them in role as the client, and they will respond in the first person from role. If they need to say something from their own role they need to come back to their own chair. These firm rules underpin the hygiene of the method – each role is located in space.

Role-Taking

The supervisee moves across to the chair and embodies the client, finding their posture, gestures and breathing patterns. This usually happens with immediacy and intuitively. The supervisor can help with the process by greeting them in role and asking questions such as: "What are you wearing today?", as well as basic information questions about age, such as how long they have been working with the supervisee.

Interview-in-Role

The supervisor then conducts an interview-in-role, asking the 'client' about their experience of the therapy or the working relationship under question. Using the example of the first supervisory question above, on whether to work towards an ending, the interview-in-role might look like this.

Hello, Claire. How long have you been working with Thea? ... and what brought you to therapy in the first place? How's it been? Would it surprise you to know that Thea is wondering about whether it is time to work towards an ending?

The supervisee in role as Claire answers these questions and may add other reflections as they deepen their sense of the client's experience. Note that when addressing the supervisee in role the supervisor consistently uses "you" rather than "he/she/they" and when talking about the therapist or coach they use the third person.

The responses that the supervisee comes up with from role tend to come from a deep or deepening sense of the other. We often know something in role as the other that we do not know consciously in our own role. For this reason, an effective interview-in-role can be quite short, and the supervisor keeps an eye and an ear open for the moment when it is enough, when the exploration has served the supervisory question. The supervisor holds the supervisee in mind throughout, avoiding any temptation to become the therapist or coach to the supervisee's client. It is more like couples' work, where the attention is on the relationship between the couple and their dynamic, in this case the relationship between supervisee and their client.

Instruction to Derole

At this point the supervisee is directed to derole. The supervisor might say something like, "Thank you, Claire. Thea, come back to your own role", whilst indicating the chair they vacated at the start of the role exploration. For hygiene reasons this is a clear instruction (not a negotiation or invitation) to return to their own chair, usually accompanied with a hand gesture. Where the role has been challenging or sticky, they can be encouraged to briefly shrug off the role or pat themselves to return to their own role as they return to their own chair.

Reflection in the Here-and-Now

The supervisor asks the supervisee what they discovered, experienced or felt in role and where they are now in terms of their supervisory question.

Finally, they are asked to derole the chair that held the role of the client, by placing it back where it was originally and returning to the dyadic conversation between supervisor and supervisee without the 'as if' presence of the client.

This is the simplest version of role work. It reflects a simple arc of going into and out of the creative action method. Where there is sufficient expertise, the supervisor can direct role dialogues between therapist and client or multiple role reversals with a wider system. These extensions to the basic method of interview-in-role need to be taught and coached in action. The possibilities are limitless, but all depend on each role having a clearly defined space in the room (whether a chair, a cushion or a zone) and the supervisor using a directive style in delivering the instructions to "reverse roles", "tell him/her/them" and "derole" as a matter of psychological hygiene.

Figure 5.1 Working with role

There follow two examples of the use of role reversal in team supervision.

Example 4   Simple role reversal in team supervision

The team consists of practitioners working both therapeutically and as social workers with children and families. Polly has just started working with a new client, a ten-year-old girl, Tessa. Tessa has been referred, amongst other things, for soiling. She is invited to introduce the client to the team, not by talking about her, but by finding a space in the room to 'be' her, to move into her role.

She chooses a chair and spends a few moments finding the physicality of the girl, her way of sitting, and her posture and facial expression. Initially, the supervisor asks a few open questions to Polly as Tessa, to get her more fully into the 'as if' of the role. "What are you wearing today?" "Tell me about something you like doing." "Who lives at home with you?"

As Polly becomes settled into the role, the team members also ask questions, with a view to eliciting both basic information (Eye One material) about Tessa and also more dynamic information about the family relationships, her history, and how she is experiencing the therapy she has recently started with Polly (Eye Three and Eye Four perspectives).

The value of this process for the whole team is that they develop a felt sense of the client and her situation. Since it is Polly who is embodying the role, they also witness something of the relationship and its challenges in how Polly takes the role. Their questions allow Polly to contact what she senses about her client, as well as what she knows, and to view school, the family and the therapy through the eyes of the client.

Where there are Eye Three and Four concerns about the therapeutic relationship the questions can be geared towards shining a light specifically on this aspect of the work, for example, "Do you know why you are seeing Polly?" "What do you do in the sessions?" and "How is that for you?"

Although the technique is very simple, it has impact and immediacy since it is an invitation to open up to and feel with the internalised client. For this reason, it is important to allow time and space to derole, in this case for Polly to come back to her own chair and her own posture, and to reflect on the experience of holding the role and of responding to the questions of the supervisor and team. She may even gain some sense of what is contributing to the soiling.

Example 5 The use of Multiple Role Reversal in team supervision

On this occasion Polly (see Example 4) has a more specific supervisory question: how to understand Tessa's symptoms and issues in the context of the family and family history. This is an Eye One, Eye Three and Eye Seven question; that is, it relates to the story of the client, the therapeutic relationship and the wider context.

She is invited to place cushions on the floor to represent the members of the family system, in spatial relationship with each other as far as she is able. There are three children, of which Tessa is the middle child, and three generations, including a stepfather and estranged father and a recently deceased maternal grandmother. She reverses role with each member of the family in turn, making a statement in the first person about their place in the family, their perspective on key events in the family history and their implicit message to Tessa.

The role of Tessa is held by one of her team members while Polly explores all the other roles. She then reverses back into the role of Tessa and hears some of the key messages delivered by the team members who step into role briefly as members of the wider family system.

Reflections on the impact of the system are made both in-role and after deroling in discussion. Both Tessa and the team members have had access to the complexity of the family system, which deepens the understanding of the pressures Tessa experiences. They are able to reflect supportively with Polly on how she experiences the therapeutic relationship and how the therapy fits into the wider picture of Tessa's life.

The Psychodramatic Technique of the Double and Its Use in Supervision

In Moreno's theory of child development, the stage of the double is the earliest developmental stage. It relates to the phase where there is no differentiation, no sense of self or other. He calls this the "matrix of identity" (Moreno, 1952: 130). During this phase the infant is dependent on those around it, particularly the mother or mother figure, to attune and to be alongside it, translating its physical and vocal expressions into meaning and responding to its needs. The good-enough carer is in this sense acting as the double for the child. In classical psychodrama as a psychotherapy method, we often ask the protagonist to choose a double, someone from the group. This person will be alongside them and match their physical movements and their breathing and gestures as a way of feeling their way into the thoughts and emotions being experienced. They help the protagonist articulate their experience in the 'as if' of the psychodramatic scene, lending their ego to that of the protagonist as a mother figure lends their ego to the infant. It can be a profoundly supportive technique and one that evidences the capacity of the individual for deep empathy and attunement. The double speaks and moves 'as if' the protagonist, enabling an internal dialogue and facilitating expression to the other on the psychodramatic stage, including words which express the felt sense and the subtext of the relationship. This process is relational and two-way, the protagonist in turn opening herself responsively to the double.

In supervision we might ask ourselves to what extent our supervisee is able to internally double their client or their group. After all, when working as a therapist, part of us deeply attunes to the client, even while we hold the position of the other, in dialogue. It is as if part of us were imaginatively sitting alongside the client.

Example 6   The Double as technique within one-to-one supervision

Let us return to Patrick (see Example 3 above). He is concerned about his ongoing dissatisfaction about the relationship with his client, Celia. He is invited to place two chairs in the supervision space to symbolise the relationship. He spends some time exploring whether the two chairs are facing each other directly obliquely and finds himself changing his mind about the distance between them. At first, they seem to be very close, perhaps as a function of his feeling overwhelmed as described above. Then, he moves them further apart with Celia's chair alternating between facing him and turning away from him. "It's like there are two Celias, one that wants to stop me perceiving her by being too close, and one that stops me perceiving her by looking the other way".

In the end he uses three chairs, one for himself and two for Celia, representing these two aspects of her. He is invited to stand behind each of the two chairs or ways of being (roles) of his client and speak the subtext of her communication to him as the double of each of these roles. Standing behind the closer position he says:

Patrick, listen to all my stories, let me fill you with them 'til there is no room for you to think...there's the conflict with my boyfriend, and that boss of mine, and do you remember what I told you about mum, well the latest is ...

He spontaneously stretches out his hand towards the therapist chair with a "Halt, don't come closer!" gesture.

When he doubles the other way of being of the client, located in the second chair for her, he looks pensive, lowers his head and looks sad. Feeling his way into this aspect of the client he says:

I am frightened of being known, of intimacy. I'm looking in a different direction. You think I don't want to let you in, Patrick, but you're wrong.

I need to know you see me, even though I am hiding. You need to be patient. Help me trust!

By doubling both aspects of the client, Patrick moves beyond what he is aware of knowing and is surprised at the clarity of what he gets in touch with from the position of doubling the apparently more distant, hiding role. He returns to his own chair in the supervision space and reflects on the delicacy of his task and how he needs to hold in mind Celia's vulnerability and fear of intimacy, but also her desire to be known. It is worth noting how in doubling each of the roles of the client it is the spontaneous bodily gesture and posture that helps him articulate the subtext of her communication.

Figure 5.2 Working with the double

The Mirror Technique in Supervision

In Moreno's theory of child development, the second phase after the phase of the double is that of the mirror. At this point, the child is able to recognise herself as an object, a person, a being with boundaries and a self (see also Lacan, 1949). This is a necessary precursor for the child before being able to reverse roles with others, an important step in the capacity to mentalise. As a psychodramatic technique, the mirror position is used when the protagonist is invited to view and experience a scene or an interaction on the stage from the third position, that of an audience. Psychologically, this relates to the observing ego, the part of self that is capable of witnessing self in action.

Most of the creative supervision techniques described in this book relate to the mirror position. The Small World technique (Chapter 4) in particular uses aesthetic distance to place the supervisee in the mirror position looking at a miniature version of their professional enquiry. The mirror position helps us move from absorption and identification *within* a dynamic to a perspective *on* the dynamic. From this perspective, it is possible to consider possible responses and to contemplate change.

While there are a number of examples of the mirror position and its usefulness in the chapter on the Small World technique I include an example here of its use within a group supervision, where it is combined with role work to good effect.

Example 7   Use of Mirror technique in group supervision

Sarah is part of a supervision group from diverse therapeutic disciplines. She brings a dilemma about a conflict in a college staff team and asks the group for support. Her supervisory question is "What is going on between me and my junior colleague that leaves me feeling undermined and sidestepped, and what can I do about it?"

As she unpacks the dynamic verbally it becomes apparent that it could take a long time to explain the structural and interpersonal dynamics of the situation, the multiple projects that she manages, and the different staff groupings involved. To keep it concise she is invited instead to name the key players in the dynamic and to make a sculpt, using other group members to represent these players and the system that is being co-created. She is to pay attention to the proxemics and the underlying messages from each person in the dynamic, using posture, gesture and one message. In concrete terms she models the position and posture of each role as she brings her colleagues from the supervision group onto the stage. She then doubles the key message/ subtext for each role and steps back to witness the dynamic in action.

What emerges on the stage is an image of Sarah, supposedly in a position of leadership trying to guide and support her small team of therapists but being undermined by a member of the senior management team of the college, who is enthralled by one of the junior therapists and is now treating him as if he were in charge of the department. There is an exciting and flattering impact on the junior therapist in question, but a confusion for the other therapists in the team, and spatially Sarah appears to be being pushed further and further to the periphery.

She is invited to walk around the sculpt, viewing each person's part in the dynamic, reflecting on what their work roles are supposed to be, what the formal hierarchy is and what appears to be happening interpersonally.

She appreciates expressing the situation in three dimensions and being able to view it from different angles. She wonders out loud where she can best intervene because something must change. Before the piece of work, she had assumed that she would need an encounter with the charismatic junior colleague, but as she looks at the image of herself in the sculpt, deflated, dejected and in danger of abandoning her authority she has an insight and makes a statement to herself, that is, the Sarah on the stage.

> Stand up and face into the dynamic! You are turning away because what is happening is embarrassing, and you are using the strategy of shrinking away that you used as a child whenever there was potential conflict in the family. That's no longer appropriate. You have a right and a duty to deal with this situation. Turn back and discuss what's going on with the member of the senior management team. That's your starting point!

At this point she is invited to reverse roles with the Sarah on the stage and to make a brief statement from role to the senior management colleague and her team members, in the spirit of role training. In essence this is a rehearsal for a potential conversation to be had.

Once the sculpt is deroled and the group moves into a reflective phase there is rich role feedback from the group members holding the postures and positions of the key players in the sculpt. This is followed by a sharing of resonances from the wider supervision group about authority, status and interpersonal relationships at work.

There is an important difference in emphasis between the immersive use of interview-in-role as described above and the use of sculpting and the mirror position to gain reflective distance as described here. Both approaches use psychodramatic techniques but for contrasting purposes. The former accentuates the felt sense, from which important insights might arise, while the latter externalises the emotional situation and frees up space for thoughtfulness and considered strategic thinking.

The Use of Role and Double in Online Supervision

Working with role can be simply adapted to online supervision sessions. The supervisee will need an extra chair in the supervision space and the ability to position it within the space so both chairs can be clearly seen by the supervisor – or to be able to adjust the position of the camera sufficiently to allow good visual access for the supervisor. It is helpful to have a cloth available to place on the 'role chair' and to remove after the intervention. This gives an extra dimension and clarity to the process of deroling. If there is poor internet connectivity and/or no access to a separate chair I would discourage the use of the method.

As with the online application of all creative methods there is the added issue of the impact of the work being left in the supervisee's work or living space. The supervisory dyad should consider this together before doing an in-depth piece of role work, particularly so when the 'other' (client or colleague) is strongly negatively cathected.

In these circumstances there is a useful variation in which an empty chair is placed not in the supervisee's space, but in the supervisor's, where it can be clearly visible to the supervisee. The supervisor moves alongside and to the side, so that they can still be seen and heard, but for the duration of the role encounter the empty chair is centre screen from the point of view of the supervisee and the supervisee is instructed to focus their gaze on the imagined person in the chair.

I have also used this adaptation to helpful effect particularly to help a supervisee address disturbing material, such as news of a suicide, sudden ruptures or in an encounter with a violent other. No role reversal takes place, but the supervisor can encourage the supervisee to address the absent other 'as if' they were on the empty chair. This has the advantage of distance for the supervisee in that they can see the supervisor deroling and removing the chair.

In terms of the use of the double in online supervision there are a couple of possibilities. There needs to be enough space for the supervisee to stand behind their own or the role chair and still be seen and heard by the supervisor. The invitation might be to move into position as the double, of self or other, and to speak the subtext or the words that are not being spoken in the actual encounter. This can be quite a visceral experience, giving the supervisee an opportunity to embody and locate in space the difference between the social interaction and the potential or desired underlying communication. The technique of the double can offer the chance to speak in a raw uncensored way, whilst acknowledging that the raw communication will need to be adapted for the reality of a professional social encounter.

Another version of doubling is when the supervisor doubles for the supervisee in role or in their own role in encounter. This is delivered as an aside. It is important to check if the doubling statement is correct and to encourage the supervisee to ignore it, correct it or take on the parts that do fit, and repeat them or revise them in the role encounter. I tend to use this if I sense the supervisee is inhibited in speaking the less socially acceptable parts of their truth.

Conclusion

I have introduced the basic concepts of psychodramatic role theory and reflected on the relevance of those concepts to supervision practice. In some ways these theories are relevant to each of the techniques outlined in Part II of the book, as they form the philosophical underpinning of the LCP Creative Supervision Diploma training. I have given some examples of the use of the psychodramatic techniques of role, double and mirror to individual and group supervision practice and indicated how role work can be included in online supervision.

Note

1 Some of this chapter (within sections 'Definition of Role' to 'The psychodramatic technique of the double and its use in supervision') is an amended and updated version of material from *Creative Supervision across Modalities: Theory and applications for therapists, counsellors and other helping professionals*, edited by Anna Chesner and Lia Zografou, Copyright © Jessica Kingsley Publishers 2014, reproduced with permission of the Licensor through PLSclear.

References

Bustos, D., 1994. "Wings and Roots". In Holmes, P., Karp, M., and Watson, M., eds., *Psychodrama Since Moreno.* Routledge.

Chesner, A., and Zografou, L., 2014. *Creative Supervision across Modalities.* Jessica Kingsley.

Lacan, J., 1949. "The Mirror Stage". In Lacan, J., 1977. *Ecrits.* Routledge.

Moreno, J.L., 1952, in Fox, J. ed., 1987. *The Essential Moreno.* Springer.

Moreno, J.L., 1987a. "The Role Concept, A Bridge Between Psychiatry and Sociology". In J. Fox. ed., *The Essential Moreno.* Springer.

Moreno, J.L., 1987b. "Psychodramatic Production Techniques". In J. Fox ed., *The Essential Moreno.* Springer.

Van der Kolk, B., 2015. *The Body Keeps the Score.* Penguin.

Chapter 6

Supervising Groups and Teams

Anna Chesner

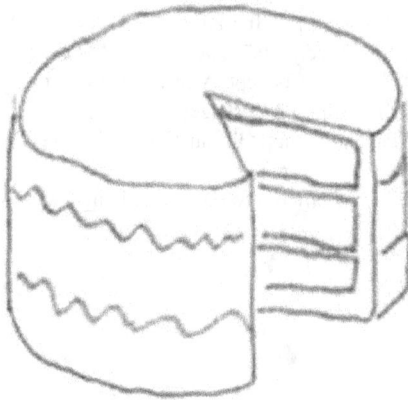

Figure 6.0

Slicing the Cake and Some Reflections on the Nature of Group

Is group supervision a good thing?

Supervisors need to draw on different and specific competencies when supervising groups. When we introduce our approach to supervising groups on the LCP training course, we begin with a sociometric exploration of the trainee supervisors' own experiences of being supervised in a group setting. On the positive side, we regularly hear an appreciation of the peer learning that can happen in a group setting by being exposed to the dilemmas of other practitioners and hearing the solutions or reflections of colleagues who bring diverse perspectives. There is a richness to be found in the breadth of the group's experience. On the negative side it seems quite common for group supervision to evoke feelings of frustration based on a number of factors: a sense that there is not enough time or space for the individual concerns of the supervisee; an experience that the supervisor

DOI: 10.4324/9781003435655-9

favours particular group members or particular themes in the group; and interpersonal dynamics that are inadequately contained and that contribute to a felt sense of lack of safety and compromised trust.

We have noted that more experienced practitioners seem more able to make positive use of the group setting. The performance anxiety and need for reassurance that accompany IDM Level 1 supervisees may contribute to making a group setting feel more exposing (Stoltenberg and McNeill, 2010). The time constraints that go with needing to share space with others can lead to feelings of unfairness for these less experienced practitioners.

How to Approach Supervising a Group

What can the supervisor do to mitigate against these potentially frustrating dynamics and foster the possibility of gaining from the more positive side of group supervision? The principles of transparency and clear contracting are crucial. There are several options as to how the group time can be allocated and we use the metaphor of a cake to consider these.

What are the ingredients of the supervisory cake? The group itself forms the bowl or container for the supervisory process and each group member brings their own ingredients (work issues) to be reflected upon in the group. While the supervisor can be seen as the head chef, in more successful supervision groups the active reflective function is held by all group members. Indeed, one of the frustrations of group supervision is often named as the supervisor supervising individuals in turn, while other group members feel that they are in a queue, waiting for their moment to get to the cake. In more successful group supervision experiences the group itself is an essential and enriching supervisory agent.

Of the five key roles of the supervisor, namely Teacher, Facilitator, Consultant, Evaluator and Administrator (see Chapter 3 on an integrated theory of supervision) it is the administrator role that can make all the difference in creating a healthy supervision group culture. The currency to be considered is time and attention. To return to the metaphor of the cake, how will it be sliced? There are active choices, which need to be contracted for in the group, both in terms of a general working contract for the group and potentially also session by session. Most supervisors in training bring an unconscious assumption, or cultural conserve, about the most effective way to slice the cake, based on their own experiences as a trainee or supervisee in group settings. We prefer to make the choices explicit so that they can be consciously considered in the light of the particular setting of the supervision group.

Here are some of the options to be thought about when choosing how the cake will be sliced or time allocated.

- Equally between supervisees, attended to one by one. This equates to the perfectly cut cake, where each portion is predictable in terms of its size. It may be a useful norm for supervision of trainees, as it allows the supervisor, in their evaluator role, to become aware of any major causes for concern. In situations where the group members are at a similar level in terms of their lack of experience and learning needs, cutting the cake in this way may offer a good learning environment, as all supervisees may be facing similar challenges and holding similar questions. There are also a couple of challenges with this approach. Firstly, if the supervisor is seduced into giving more than the set time to each person, perhaps because an issue arises that is a red flag or of a higher complexity than can be managed in the time allocated, then there will be repercussions in the group dynamic, as somebody else will lose out on their slice and be left with crumbs and go hungry. Secondly, the time constraint may lead to a lack of any in-depth exploration of the work, which can bring its own frustrations to the group. Thirdly, it relies on the supervisees being able to discern what is pertinent to bring to the group. Such discernment grows with experience and may not be highly developed in a neophyte practitioner, who in their concern for their own performance and 'getting it right' may fail to attend to other factors which then emerge in the group and require more time than has been allocated.

- In a rota system, whereby one or more supervisees present their work, more or less formally in a pre-arranged sequence. They get the large slices of cake, but the rest of the group know that their turn will also come and so there is a predictable fairness in the system. An advantage of this approach is the predictability of getting the attention of the group over a period of time. Those who are presenting have the chance to really consider what they need from the group and to review their notes and their own thinking ahead of the presentation. Some structured time can be allocated at the beginning of the supervision session to hear back from the previous presenter/s in terms of how they have made use of the supervision. There are some interesting refinements of this approach, such as that described in The Art of Relational Supervision (Hargaden, 2015) whereby there is a clear and timed ritual process for the presentation, the group's associations and reflections on it, their reflections on the group process, theoretical reflections and a dialogue with the presenter. Potential disadvantages of this system are that there is a lack of flexibility to respond to more urgent needs that have arisen; it may be more suited to those who take a more academic approach to case presentation; there may be some acting out in terms of some group members being absent when less popular presenters are scheduled on the rota or absence from a presenter who may be avoiding the spotlight and the scrutiny of the group.

- Identifying a group concern, either sociometrically (i.e. through the spatial and embodied expression of thematic resonances at that moment) or through discussion, and the person who holds that group concern explores it on behalf of and with the support of the group. This equates to a large slice of cake being allocated to one person, but with the investment of the group in their work. The advantage of this approach is that the group is active in the choice of focus for that particular session and that focus arises spontaneously in response to the moment. Since they have been active in the choice made, they also get to reflect at the end on how the work was meaningful to them, so there is an interesting interplay between group and individual focus. The supervisee has the opportunity to explore their theme in depth and with plenty of time for facilitated creative interventions. Disadvantages are that sociometric choices, whilst they are ostensibly made in terms of the theme presented, can also be used to exclude those whose communication style is more challenging for the group. The approach may be more suited to a mature group, where members can tolerate not getting a personal slice of cake for a period of time, in the knowledge that all group members can learn from each other. It may also be supportive in a team setting, where a number of team members may be dealing with similar systemic issues from different perspectives.

- By the group as a whole exploring a key theme from multiple perspectives concurrently. This approach relies on a good warm-up phase to identify common themes in the group. It features the supervisor in their facilitator role, and group members have a high degree of autonomy in how they use the facilitation to explore their own supervisory question around the common theme. Advantages are that the group is actively involved both in the choice of theme and in their own exploration of it. They all have full access to the cake. It can be challenging to identify a common theme, and it is important for the supervisor not to force the issue if a common theme does not present itself. The approach is also dependent on the supervisor being able to offer a creative structure related to the theme or to hold a free-floating dialogue in the group that is guided back to the agreed common theme. For both these reasons this approach relies on a good degree of spontaneity on the part of the supervisor. We cannot usually decide a priori that we will work with a common theme.

- Negotiating who needs how big a slice of the cake at the start of the session and allocating time accordingly. This approach has the advantage of being flexible and responsive to the stated needs and wishes of the group. It does, however, rely on group members being able to discern what is urgent and important and how much time realistically would be required to do justice to their needs. The supervisor needs to keep an independent eye on what he or she regards as realistic and be prepared to challenge where someone habitually underestimates their own need for time and attention.

- Some combination of the above. Being aware of the different options gives the supervisor a frame of reference to make informed choices and to be mindful of the implication of the choices made. Some settings may insist on an externally determined norm. For example, some counselling or therapy trainings may require formal case presentations in a rota system so the training organisation can meet certain academic, assessment or practice requirements. The principle of transparency is helpful in these circumstances, in terms of acknowledging where the group has choice and where the parameters are predetermined. Where the group has more autonomy in determining how the cake will be sliced it can be helpful to hold in mind the upsides and downsides of sticking to the same approach in a reliable fashion. I favour a short check-in at the start of a session to take the temperature of the group and to negotiate the use of time.

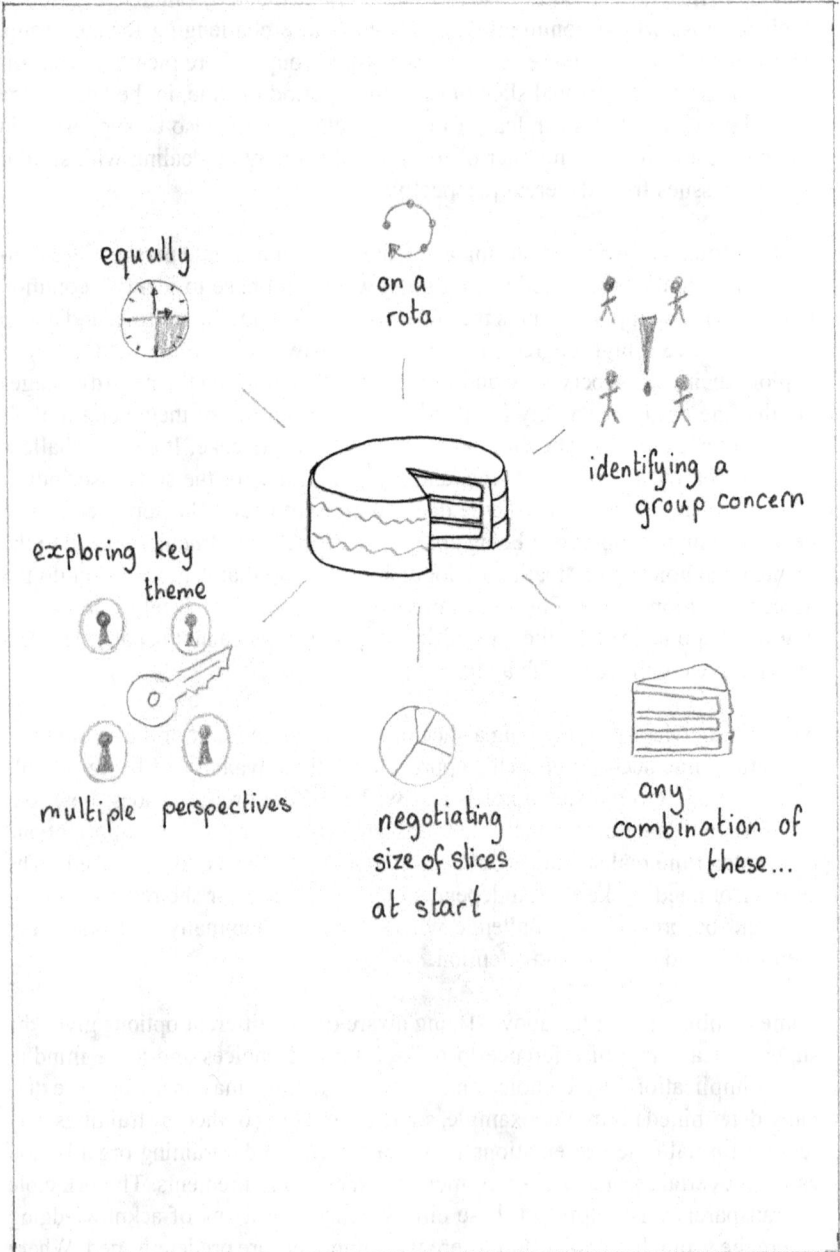

Figure 6.1 Slicing the Cake

The Role of the Supervisor

Group dynamics are a powerful factor, for better or for worse. With this in mind, the principles of transparency and fairness are more fundamental than the choice of creative technique used in group supervision. A reflective group that is 'just talking' will be more creative and useful to participants than a group where the supervisor focuses on their own facilitation of a creative structure at the cost of attending to how they are conducting the group session in terms of the supervisory needs of the group.

Let us consider the five roles of the supervisor as applied to group supervision.

Supervisor as Administrator

The supervisor as administrator attends to the norms of the group, clarifies an agreement about these and is vigilant when there is a breach. When dealing with a group, with its complex dynamics the supervisor as administrator cannot afford to be passive in this respect. We need to attend to (and model) punctual and regular attendance and clarity of communication around any absences or lateness. These have more impact in a group than in a one-to-one setting. If the group is veering from its task of reflecting on practice by attempting to go more into a personal therapy agenda or to act out political or interpersonal rivalries the supervisor does well to notice this and to name it. We may inquire if what is going on is helpful and in line with the agreed contract of the group or point out that there is a discrepancy between the contract and the direction the group is going. The supervisor is responsible for timekeeping within the session, so that, whatever techniques are used, these are used succinctly and hygienically, with adequate attention to the arc of a session. The supervisor 'holds' the group by attending to administrative factors. Neglecting to do so may raise an anxiety in the group about 'who is minding the shop?' Neophyte supervisors and those with limited experience of holding groups may be reluctant to step into the authority of the administrator role in the group setting. It is an important competency that creates space for the reflective work to be done.

Supervisor as Teacher

The role of teacher can be shared within the group. Even when supervisees are relative beginners in their professional careers it is helpful to open possibilities for peer learning and sharing of practice, clinical wisdom and relevant life experience to all group members. The supervisor can also step cleanly, transparently and unapologetically into the role of teacher where this will be helpful. We may demonstrate a technique or depict our view of a situation and share our own theoretical understanding. The important thing is to know that we are stepping into the teacher role, so that we can also step out of it and pass the spotlight onto the other group members, to reflect on what has been shared and process it in their own terms.

Supervisor as Facilitator

What is it that is facilitated within a group supervision? This includes structures for checking in, for the articulation of individual needs, negotiating the division of time and warming up to the themes that are present. These tasks facilitate the work of the group. Any creative techniques used in the warming up, action or closure phase are facilitation tasks, and the supervisor needs to find a spacious, inviting and clear tone for these parts of the session and to hold in mind the timing of these. Preparation for the closure of the session is both an administration and a facilitation task, a time when any creative materials are deroled and when the focus is on the transition between the exploratory work and the identification of action tasks or reflective takeaways for group members.

Supervisor as Consultant

A consultancy relationship in supervision is the most egalitarian. While the supervisor holds the frame and brings their own competencies, experience and practice wisdom into the space, it is understood that their perspective is one view amongst several and does not have hierarchical dominance. A group that can run on a consultancy basis tends to be a mature group, where the supervisory and reflective task is understood to be held by all. The added value of the supervisor rests in being somewhat on the outside, while still being part of the group, holding the space for the work to be done, and reflecting on the meta-level of the group process.

Supervisor as Evaluator

As in one-to-one supervision the evaluator function of the group supervisor is indispensable. In their noticing risk factors and learning opportunities in the work presented, along with the developmental levels and needs of individual participants, the supervisor also evaluates the dynamic of the group. In training settings, the supervisor may have formal evaluative reports to write. Some employers also require a periodic progress report. These tasks inevitably accentuate a power or status differential in the group that could lead to mistrust or group members wishing to present their successes rather than their authentic challenges. It is helpful to name and be transparent about the evaluative function of the supervisor so that it does not become a taboo subject or a hidden agenda. Where possible evaluation can be an inclusive task and group members can be affirmed for their ability to self-evaluate and peer evaluate in a balanced and congruent way. If this capacity is regarded as a competency in its own right, group supervisees will be more motivated to reflect non-defensively and support each other in developing a balanced group culture.

A Note on Group Dynamics

Supervisors who are familiar with group theory and the practical tasks of managing groups are at an advantage when approaching the task of group supervision. There are some useful group theoretical concepts to be held in mind which are briefly named here.

Foulkes' Concept of the Group Matrix

Foulkes, who developed group analytic psychotherapy, used the term 'matrix' to refer to the complex web of relationships and communications both conscious and unconscious that are active in a group (Foulkes, 1984). It is helpful for the group supervisor to keep in mind this web of communication and resonance that is active in a group process. It is a useful concept in terms of the groupness of group. A group is more than the sum of its parts. As a concept it is compatible with Moreno's idea of tele (see Chapter 3), the felt sense of attraction, aversion or neutrality between people, which underpins the practice of sociometry in small and large groups.

Tuckman's Developmental Sequence in Small Groups (Tuckman, 1965)

Tuckman identifies four stages of group process – forming, storming, norming and performing. A fifth stage of adjourning or mourning was later added. The way in which these stages manifest in a supervision group can be profoundly affected by the setting up and contracting process at the start of the work. The more clarity and transparency there is in the contracting phase, the more buy-in there will be by the group participants, and the less entrenched any storming dynamics become.

Storming is a process which may be about testing the safety of the group through pushing the agreed or less explicit boundaries. This can feel challenging and indeed is intended to be so. A key competency for the group supervisor is to be able to stand back from such challenges and to reflect on them with curiosity and openness. Storming may be a useful opportunity for clarifying group needs and norms. The way the supervisor responds to such a dynamic can be a powerful role modelling for supervisees when they themselves are faced with challenges and conflicts. The danger of not meeting the dynamic of storming is that conflicts which are not addressed seldom go away. In a worst-case scenario, the group becomes an anti-group (Nitsun, 1996) dominated by destructive forces. If dealt with, the same dynamics can be transformed into creative developmental solutions.

Norming is the stage when a group settles into its norms and moves towards performing, in the sense of doing the work it is there for.

Adjourning or mourning is the phase in which the end of the group is felt and explicitly prepared for and addressed. It is worth noting that when a group changes its membership it is in effect a new group, so even an ongoing group will have moments of adjourning or mourning.

Bion's Group Theory

Bion's concepts on the nature and function of groups can also be helpful to the group supervisor. He contrasts the healthy functioning of a 'work' group with three kinds of 'basic assumption' groups, fuelled by unconscious anxieties and attempted solutions to these (Bion, 1998). The first of these, the *basic assumption dependency* group is one where all the solutions are invested in a leader and group members are passive and obedient to the leader's guidance. A supervisor might notice this in a group where, despite the invitation to reflect, members are silent and focused on the supervisor or one participant to give answers. The second of these, the *basic assumption fight/flight* group operates on the level of a perceived danger or emergency. In a supervision group this might manifest as passive or active attacks on the task of supervision or against the supervisor or other colleagues in the group. The third of the basic assumption groups is called *basic assumption pairing* and involves the unconscious fantasy of a couple in the group producing a saviour or messiah. In a supervision group this might involve two group members being invested with higher status in the group, being left to do all the work or being looked to for the answers.

Later developments of Bion's theory have added the idea of *basic assumption oneness*, as manifested in cults, where there is a merging and a lack of differentiation in a group (Turquet, 1974); *basic assumption me-ness*, where there is a denial of group and each person sees themselves as an isolated system (Lawrence, Bain and Gould, 1996); and *basic assumption purity/pollution* (Chattopadhyay, 2018), in which group members distance themselves from a perceived source of pollution, which might be an idea or those holding a certain idea in a group in order to hold onto the purity of a previous orthodoxy.

All the above concepts are worthy of further study by those supervising groups and are offered here in brief as a stimulus to further reflection.

References

Bion, W.R., 1998. *Experiences in Groups: and Other Papers.* Routledge.

Chattopadhyay, G., 2018. "The Sixth Basic Assumption baPu (Basic Assumption Purity/Pollution)". In *Organisational and Social Dynamics*, *18*, 103–121.

Foulkes, S.H., 1984. *Therapeutic Group Analysis.* Karnac.

Hargaden, H. ed., 2015. *The Art of Relational Supervision: Clinical Implications of the Use of Self in Group Supervision.* Routledge.

Lawrence, W., Bain, A., and Gould, L., 1996. "The Firth Basic Assumption". In *Free Associations, 6* Part 1 (37), 2855.

Nitsun, M., 1996. *The Anti-Group: Destructive Forces in the Group and Their Creative Potential.* Routledge.

Stoltenberg, C.D., and McNeill, B.W., 2010. *IDM Supervision, an Integrative Developmental Model for Supervising Counselors and Therapists.* Routledge.

Tuckman, B., 1965. "Developmental sequence in small groups". In *Psychological Bulletin, 63*, 384–99.

Turquet, P.M., 1974. "Leadership: The Individual and the Group". In Gibbard. G.S. et al, eds. *The Large Group: Therapy and Dynamics.* Jossey Bass.

Chapter 7

Creative Techniques in Group Supervision

Anna Chesner

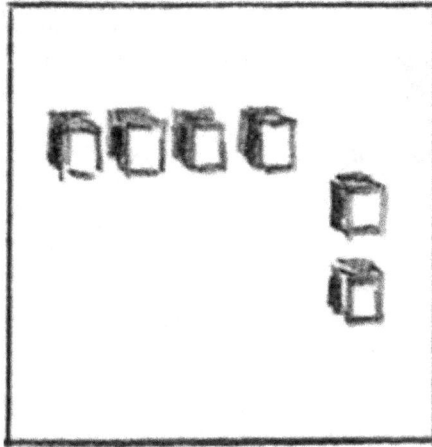

Figure 7.0

Throughout this book there are examples of creative supervisory techniques that can be used in group supervision (see Chapters 4, 5, 8, 11 and 12). In this chapter we include some creative techniques that are specific to group supervision, in particular those techniques based in Playback Theatre and Sociometry.

Playback Theatre-Inspired Creative Supervision Techniques

Playback Theatre is an improvisational form of non-scripted theatre that was developed by Jonathan Fox (2019) and Jo Salas (1993). It has gained popularity globally and there is a Centre for Playback Theatre that offers courses at core training, advanced and leadership levels. Playback performances are used in communities, conferences and organisational settings as a tool to help people and groups dialogue with each other through their personal experiences. As a ritual form it has elements

DOI: 10.4324/9781003435655-10

of clear structure which facilitate dialogue in a creative and performative way. For examples of how it has been used see Fox and Salas (2021). While it is popular with psychodrama psychotherapists, dramatherapists and other arts therapists as an adjunct to their core therapy competencies, it is not in itself a therapy and has no claims to be so. It is, however, a deeply expressive and creative discipline that is playful and that accentuates active, embodied listening and the development of expressiveness and improvisational complicity.

A Playback Theatre company trains together over time to develop spontaneity and expressiveness, so that when presented with a story told by an individual in a group, organisational or community setting, they have the ability to play off each other and reflect back the told story through a succinct improvised and spontaneous performance.

It is intrinsically a reflective discipline and one which can be adapted for purposes of group supervision. Of course, the aesthetic values of a trained playback company are of a different order than what can be expected by a non-trained supervision group. However, there can be significant benefits in a supervision group having a go at using some playback structures together and for each other. The group is both audience and actor for the 'stories' or moments of practice that individuals tell.

Key benefits are that group members deepen their listening to each other. They take momentary risks in daring to be expressive in embodied and vocal ways. They allow themselves to be surprised and to trust their own spontaneity in response to what they hear. This experience is enlivening and also promotes trust and openness within the supervision group.

Flares

This is a warmup activity that includes key elements of the Playback ritual and that focuses the group on checking in briefly at a personal level.

The group stands in a circle and each person identifies who is opposite them. The 'conductor' (the playback specific term for the holder of the ritual in all Playback forms) asks each person in the group to share a moment of their journey or a feeling that they arrive with. At that moment they are the 'teller' (the Playback specific term for the person who narrates from their own experience) and speak for a few moments. The person opposite them in the circle, and the two people on either side of that person form a cluster who listen in particular readiness to offer an enactment using body and voice, an enactment that lasts just a few seconds. The enactment is launched with the ritual invocation "Let's Watch!" by the conductor and ends with a freeze frame or still tableau when the essence of the 'story' has been brought to the stage. At that point the three actors turn their gaze to the teller, in 'acknowledgement' of their contribution and soften the still image. They are thanked and return to the regular circle. The next teller is identified, and the process continues around the circle. In this way each person gets to tell, and each person also gets to offer an acting contribution three times as part of a trio.

The whole process is succinct and serves to identify some key features of the spirit of Playback: that there is a conductor who elicits the story, a teller who shares an authentic experience with the conductor, and via the conductor with the group; that the enactment is launched by the ritual phrase "Let's Watch!"; that direct eye contact with the teller is avoided during the enactment; and that the enactment is closed with a still image that is softened as the acknowledgement is made through eye contact with the teller. There is no opportunity for discussion amongst the actors, and inevitably some enactments will be more on point than others. The succinctness and pace of the process contribute to a spirit of offering something and letting go. The idea is not to enact the full narrative of what has been shared, but each of the three performers offers something, an expression of feeling or an indication of one moment within the narrative. The fact of moving from one enactment to the next encourages swiftness of deroling and agility in shifting from one state to another. It can be a revelation for group members to have their group creativity and potential for co-operation evidenced so succinctly.

While Flares as a form is particularly suited to warming up and introducing a group to the fundamentals of other Playback forms it can also be used as a warmup to supervisory themes. In this case the conductor might give the invitation to share a moment from your practice and how you feel in response to it. While the content will not be particularly fleshed out it can serve as a first step in unpacking what individual supervisees are holding and a first step in unpacking where the supervisory focus may need to be as the session unfolds.

Four Elements

This structure is best suited for the main body of a supervision group session. It offers a ritual playback form that allows multiple issues to be heard and played back. It has its origin in a playback theatre rehearsal form developed by Francis Batten (personal communication), whereby individual playbackers could practice using art, music, movement and voice one by one for each other in a rotating sequence. Lia Zografou saw the potential for adapting the structure for group supervision and has written elsewhere (Chesner and Zografou, 2014) about how she developed this form as a way to attend to the supervisory needs of larger teams of workers who had limited access to regular supervision during economically challenging times.

It has been used successfully within both clinical and business contexts and has become a valued form within the LCP Creative Supervision Training.

Introducing Four Elements

The room is arranged as it would be for a playback theatre performance. There are four performer chairs on the stage, evenly spaced and facing directly to the audience. There is a stage area between these chairs and the audience. There are two chairs to one side, close to the audience and at an angle to the stage. One of these, closest to the audience, is for the supervisor/conductor, and the other is for the teller, closest to the stage.

In terms of props or equipment, a flipchart or similar on a stand, with pastels or felt pens, is positioned close to the first chair. Plain coloured cloths are placed by or under the second chair. One or two musical instruments can be placed by the third chair, and the fourth chair is empty.

The group needs basic instruction into the ritual of the Playback structure. Anyone from the audience can come up to the teller's chair and share what is on their mind in relation to their work: successes, challenges, reflections on how things are going in the team or organisation, and curiosities that are emerging.

Before they begin their account four group members inhabit the four chairs on the stage in readiness to respond to what they hear. The first chair is designated the 'Artist' and their way of reflecting back what they hear is through 'mark-making'. We prefer this term to 'drawing' as it is not dependent on expertise as an artist. The second chair is designated the 'Mover's' chair and the primary mode of communication here is the body, optionally supported by using cloth or cloths. The third chair is for the 'Bard' or musician and the response to the narration is through musical instruments or voice. A snippet of a known song can be sung or adapted, or the bard can create their own poem, song or story. The fourth chair is for the 'Colleague', and this person responds by sharing something authentic from their own personal or professional experience, without offering advice.

The role of the conductor is to interview the teller so that the story is elicited and heard by the group. The conductor needs to be sensitive to the emotional state of the teller and their ability to articulate what they are telling. If the teller is able to speak clearly and structures their narrative in an accessible way the conductor may not need to intervene at all other than to hold the ritual, marking the moment of transition when the enactment begins with the words "Let's Watch!" If the teller struggles with language or is not clearly audible the conductor may succinctly repeat, paraphrase or clarify the narrative. There is no demand on the conductor to work through or find solutions for any implicit or explicit supervisory question. The effectiveness of the form rests on the power of being heard and understood in a group. It is one of the few creative techniques in this book that does not explicitly pose or refine a supervisory question. The fact of being heard and understood can itself lead to a shift in the individual teller or in the group.

Each performer offers their response to the story in turn, perhaps within a few seconds or up to a minute. They are encouraged not to look directly at the teller whilst performing but to direct their gaze into the audience, the wider group. This ritual norm supports the boundary between stage and audience and gives the teller aesthetic distance from the material as it is being played back. The performers are also encouraged to mark the closure of their offer with a moment of stillness, before returning to their onstage seat and allowing the focus to move on to the next Element or performer.

After the final performer completes their offer, the conductor marks the end of this phase of the ritual with the words "Thank You" and that is the cue for those on the stage to turn their gaze towards the teller, in 'acknowledgement', as seen above in Flares.

The conductor briefly checks back with the teller by way of closure. A useful question for this phase of the process is "what are you taking away from this?" or "what are you with now, having seen these reflections?"

Once the teller has responded to this question they are released from the teller's chair and directed to return to their place in the audience, and the performers are similarly thanked and released from the stage. At this point there is an invitation for a new teller to come to the teller's chair, and the process repeats, one story often evoking another and creating a kind of dialogue through story in the group.

At the end of the structured ritual, it can be helpful to derole the space and come together in a reflective circle, to consider and summarise common themes running through the different stories, and to share which 'elements' group members enjoyed performing or found more challenging. It may be important to mark which themes and pieces of work will need to be returned to for a more in-depth exploration and what feels more resolved.

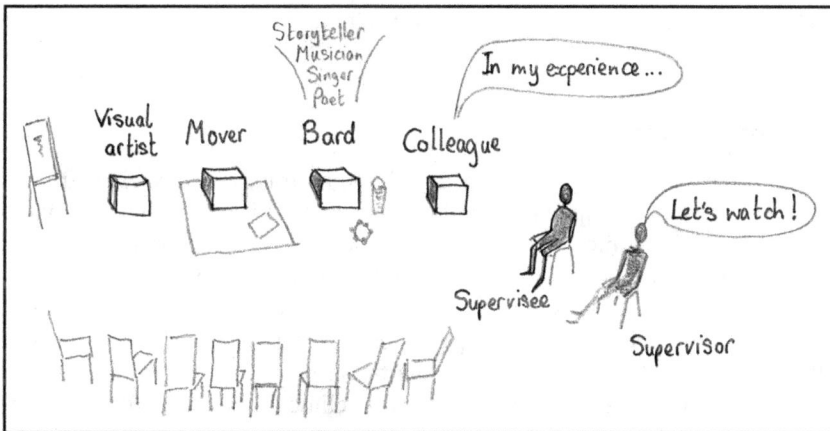

Figure 7.1 Four Elements

Variations Online

Four Elements can be adapted to online supervision. The role of the conductor as holder of the ritual remains similar but with some added responsibilities in terms of managing the online platform. When using the Zoom platform there is a choice to be made about 'pinning' or 'spotlighting' those 'onstage' to indicate where our attention is. We can also choose to use the function that allows those people whose cameras are off (e.g. the audience) to disappear from the screen. This is helpful in maximising screen space for the moments of performance. When the performers come up to the 'stage', they can use the change name function, so it is very clear who is Artist, Mover, Bard, and Colleague. The conductor and teller remain visible, and as the teller and performers are dismissed from the stage the audience is requested to return to video participation, and the performers revert to their usual screen name. Given the limitations of the online platform the conductor needs to mark the moment of acknowledgement from the performers to the teller verbally or suggest a form of gesture that the performers can make as an equivalent to making eye contact.

We have focused here on Flares and Four Elements. There are other playback theatre forms that can become part of a supervision group's repertoire of creative techniques, such as the short forms of three-part story and fluid sculptures. On the LCP Creative Supervision Training we focus on Flares and Four Elements as accessible structures within the overall purpose of supervision, but if the supervisor has specific playback theatre training there is no need to limit the group to these two forms. Playback theatre is intrinsically reflective at a group level, so if the supervisor has the relevant training and the group members are inspired by the creativity and expressiveness of playback theatre there are many options that can enliven and develop a creative supervision group.

Cycle of Change

This creative structure comes from the Morenian tradition of sociometry and involves the whole group concurrently. I came across it in a conference workshop run by Liz White, a Canadian psychodrama psychotherapist. She had adapted it from the work of Ann Hale, who worked extensively on sociometry including various versions of the Sociometric Cycle (Hale, 1985; White, 2002). We include it as a group supervision method on the LCP training as a reflective and creative structure that is particularly useful for marking endings and changes, both in the training group and in clinical and non-clinical practice settings.

Some prior preparation of the workspace is required. A four-quadrant circle (mandala) is marked with cloth or other props. It needs to be large enough for all the group members to step into and move around from one quadrant to another. The supervisor can use colour and texture to evoke a sense of the four seasons. The top right-hand quadrant represents spring, the lower right-hand quadrant represents summer, the left-hand lower quadrant represents autumn, and the top right-hand quadrant represents winter. Hale uses plus and minus signs to capture something of the process of changing relationships over time. The quadrant of spring is denoted with ++, representing the positivity and hope of that season, something of the enthusiasm of a honeymoon period in a relationship. The summer quadrant is denoted with a +-, the beginning of ambivalence, potentially also passion and conflict. The autumn quadrant is denoted with --, representing the beginning of distancing or withdrawal from what was impassioned, and the winter quadrant is denoted with a NN, denoting the neutrality of a more complete withdrawal, in readiness for a new cycle.

Hale uses the structure to represent sociometric relationships in a group, ranging from mutually positive through to mutually neutral. In White's version of this structure, she relates it to the nature of relationship and how love and belonging can change to something more ambivalent, negative and neutral, either in rapidly repeating cycles or over time (personal communication).

The supervisor begins by walking round the cycle, spending some time in each quadrant, and introducing the group to the meaning of each quadrant, perhaps using personal examples or other ways of bringing it to life. As they do this the supervision group members quietly reflect on how these stages and states resonate personally and professionally.

The next stage is to invite group members to step into the circle and spend some time in each quadrant, noticing how their body responds, the feelings that come up, and memories or current situations that are evoked. I encourage people to explore in silence and at their own pace and to ensure that they move around the full cycle at least twice, the first time focusing on resonances from their personal life, and the second time reflecting specifically on work situations. In each case it can be helpful to pay particular attention to the dynamic transitions from one quadrant to another.

The next step is for each person to land somewhere that is meaningful to them at this moment and one by one to share what the significance is and how the journey to that place was made.

The supervisor then invites group members to position themselves somewhere else on the quadrant, perhaps somewhere that was challenging for them as they journeyed round, or possibly somewhere they aspire to be. Another round of sharing takes place from that position, and group members are given the choice to conclude the exercise in that new place or to return to their previous position on the circle.

The same structure can be used for future projection, particularly if the Cycle of Change is used at the end of a training or at the end of a series of group supervision sessions. Group members are invited to imagine themselves in one-, five-, or ten-years' time and move to where they will be professionally or personally. They move to the quadrant that best represents the state they expect to be in and allow the bodily posture to reflect the new or imagined role. Each person has a moment to speak to the group from their future role embodied in the here and now.

A final group reflection takes place once everyone steps out of the circle, and the props demarcating the circle are deroled. This is a time for reflecting on the experience and for a free exchange of ideas.

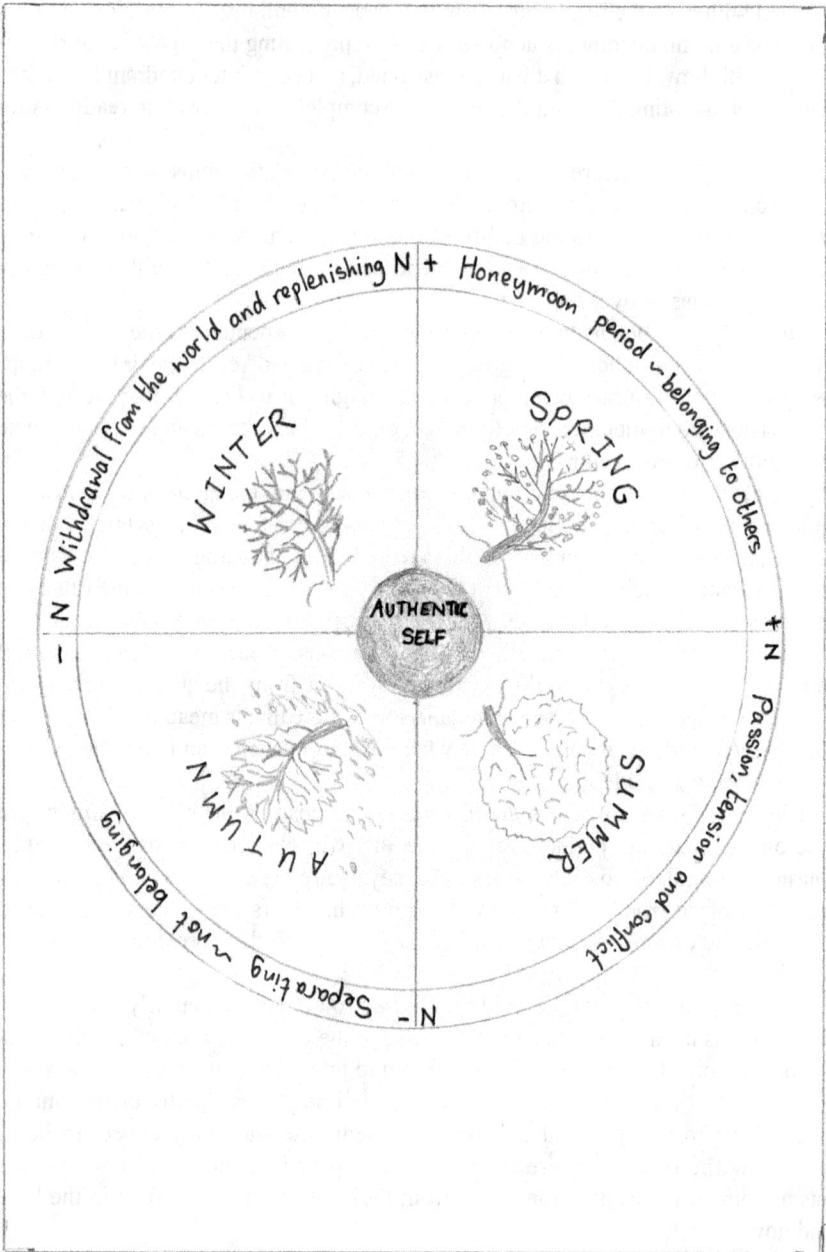

Figure 7.2 Cycle of Change

Conclusion

While this chapter has focused on some methods that have been particularly developed for group supervision these are not exclusive.

All the creative methods outlined in this book can be used within a group supervision setting. Sometimes the group may focus on one person's presentation via one of the techniques, followed by a group discussion. This might involve a small world or a Six Shape Supervision Structure (6S) or a Seven Step Relationship Sequence (7SRS) being made in the centre, witnessed by the group. At other times each individual, having identified a supervisory enquiry, explores their question simultaneously through a creative technique. This might involve group members moving within a larger FERN map (Chapter 11) or making an individual 6S. Discussion can then take place in pairs, small groups or with the group as a whole. A third option is for the group to work on one enquiry together. This is particularly suited to team supervision. The group might create its own sculpt (a larger version of Small World) collaboratively through negotiation. For further ideas on how to choose and approach any of these possibilities see Chapter 6 and for examples of each method used in group settings see Chapters 4, 5, 8, 9, 11 and 12.

References

Chesner, A., and Zografou, L., eds., 2014. *Creative Supervision across Modalities.* Jessica Kingsley Publications.

Fox, J., 2019. *Beyond Theatre.* Tusitala Publishing.

Fox, J., and Salas, J., 2021. *Personal Stories in Public Spaces: Essays on Playback Theatre by its Founders.* Tusitala Publishing.

Hale, A., 1985. *Conducting Clinical Sociometric Explorations: A Manual for Psychodramatists and Sociometrists.* Royal Publishers.

Salas, J., 1993. *Improvising Real Life.* Kendall Hunt.

White, L., 2002. *The Action Manual: Techniques for Enlivening Group Process and Individual Counselling.* Elizabeth White.

Chapter 8

The Six Shape Supervision Structure

Anna Chesner

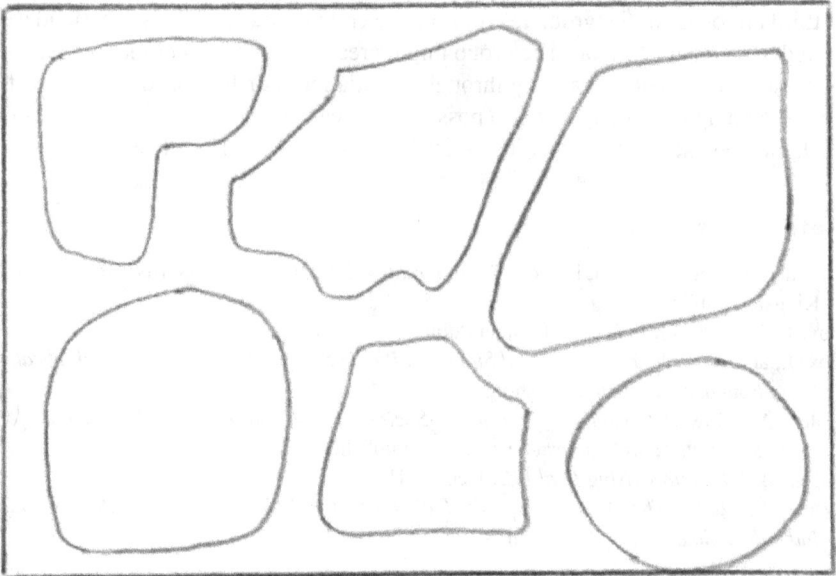

Figure 8.0

The Six Shape Supervision Structure (also shortened to 6S) is a projective, paper-based supervisory tool.[1] It is highly structured and takes the supervisee on a reflective journey through which the supervisee contemplates a supervisory enquiry through distinct lenses.

It can be used for self-supervision, one-to-one supervision and supervision in a group or team setting. It was devised specifically to suit a broad range of supervisory questions and to offer a contained and creative way for the supervisee to contemplate their inquiry prior to processing the exercise in dialogue. The value of the method rests precisely in the shifting of perspectives that it encourages.

DOI: 10.4324/9781003435655-11

I initially wrote about this method some 10 years ago (Chesner and Zografou, 2014). The version here represents a development and refinement of the structure and its facilitation as described in the earlier text.

I begin by describing the facilitation and execution of the method and then give examples of the method in practice.

Preparation

Firstly, identify the supervisory question. This is crucial as the supervisor will need to adapt the facilitation of the method to the content of the question. Make sure that the supervisory question is explicitly agreed upon. I favour writing it down. This is the first part of the arc of the session and is verbal and dialogical. The central, creative part of the session is best conducted without discussion, but with verbal prompts from the supervisor as facilitator, allowing the supervisee to immerse themselves in mark-making. The final part of the arc is again dialogical, with the supervisee talking through the images and their process, and the supervisor initially listening and then, where appropriate, engaging in further consultative dialogue. It is useful to return to the supervisory question as part of the closure.

Materials required are as follows: a large sheet of paper, A2 or A3 are recommended, as well as art materials such as pastels or paint-based pens, something that can make bold or smudged lines rather than coloured pencils which tend to be more tentative on the page.

Facilitation of the Method

I shall now introduce the structure and highlight the facilitation for each stage and its function as a reflective process.

> Divide a large sheet of paper into six irregular shapes. Each of these will provide the frame and boundary of a separate image. Make the shapes as large as you can and the space between them as small as possible.

Why irregular? Of course, the sheet could be folded or drawn into six equal rectangles and functionally this would serve the purpose to some extent. However, there is something playful about making the shapes random and more free-flowing. This serves as a warmup to spontaneity and creativity. At this point the supervisor can clarify that the technique is not about drawing ability; it is about mark-making in a way that makes some sense to the supervisee.

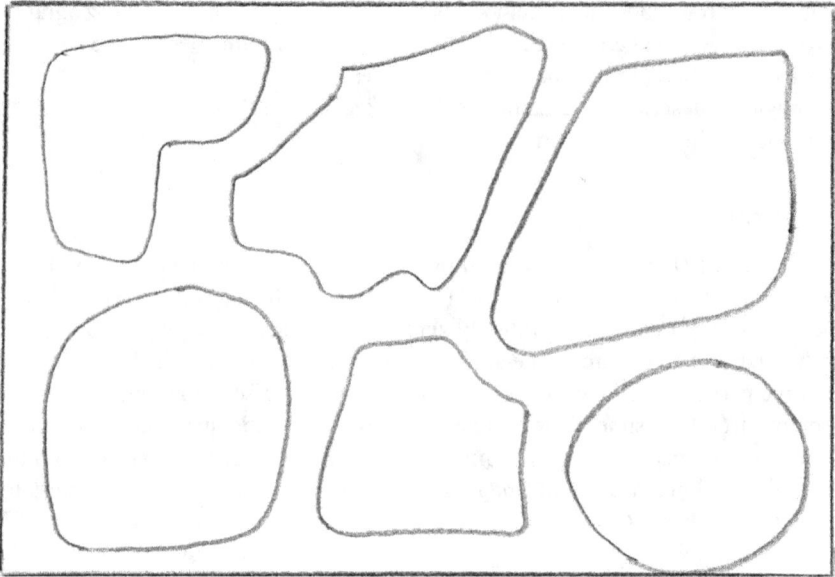

Figure 8.1 Six irregular shapes

Choose an initial shape. Consider your supervisory question and make marks
to represent that question or concern. Include everything that is relevant. It
does not need to be naturalistic; you can make marks to symbolise in your
own way what is relevant.

By reminding the supervisee of the question you can prompt the inclusion of the
relevant people, places and issues. For example, let us take the question "How can
I help my client connect with their compassion?" (Eye Two, Eye Three and Eye
Four). In this example the marks in the first shape should include the therapist, the
client, something of the therapeutic relationship and something around the absence
or disconnect from compassion. Let us take a different question: "Is it time for
me to make a change in my career?" (Eye Seven or Eye Eight). Here it would be
important to include something of the relationship between the supervisee, their
current work and the possibility of something else. In each case the dramatis per-
sonae and relevant relationships are symbolised in the first shape.

Think about your supervisory question again and consider what your goal is
and where you would like to get to with this exploration. Choose a second
shape and make an image of that goal or destination.

Again, it is helpful to articulate this invitation in terms of the specific supervisory question. For example, using the question above you might say "Make an image of what it would look like if you were able to help your client connect with their compassion?" or "Make an image of how you would like your work-life to look, or how it would look if you did make a decision one way or the other". In this way the supervisee reframes the problem or challenge articulated in the first shape as a wish or goal depicted in the second shape. This has some similarities to the use of a miracle question in brief solution-focused therapy (de Shazer, 1988).

So, what gets in the way of achieving this goal? Let us call this the obstacle. It might belong to you, the client, the system. Find a way to represent whatever it is that is blocking the achievement of this supervisory goal in a third shape. What is in the way of it looking like it does in shape two?

The supervisor can usefully frame this invitation with reference to the supervisory question. In terms of the questions above the supervisor might say, "So what's in the way that stops you helping your client connect with their compassion? Something in them, something in you, or in the therapeutic relationship? Find a way to mark this in a third shape". It can be quite helpful to give a few options and to invite the supervisee to consider the location and nature of the obstacle. The supervisor is modelling curiosity and open-mindedness and in a sense doubling (see Chapter 5) the curiosity of the supervisee. In terms of the second supervisory question above, the invitation might be, "What stops you from making a decision, or what keeps you where you are in your work?"

As you move towards the fourth shape, I am going to invite you to do something different. I invite you to symbolically take off your thinking head for a moment – place it to one side. You will be picking it up again soon, but for the moment you are invited to attend fully to your feelings about this situation. Choose a fourth shape and some colours. When you are ready, I invite you to close your eyes and use your non-dominant hand to allow the feelings onto the page. You can use your other hand to help locate where the fourth shape is.

I favour demonstrating playfully the moving of the 'thinking head' to one side at the start of this facilitation and asking the supervisee to mirror the gesture. While it might seem silly to some, if it is done with the clear intention to give space and focus to the emotional dimension of the supervisory issue it can really serve to give permission for the expression of feelings. Because the eyes are closed during the mark-making and the non-dominant hand is used the supervisee has the opportunity to channel their feelings onto the page in a non-representational way. It is interesting to listen to the sound of the art materials on the page and to notice the pressure and rhythm of the mark-making. This can be cathartic or a more investigative internal enquiry for the supervisee, a chance to really notice what they are feeling.

> Now pick up your thinking head again; you are going to need it. As you move into a fifth shape you are invited to reflect on what you know. This shape is for marking 'causes and contexts'. What do you know at a theoretical level that may be relevant to understanding your supervisory question? What has contributed to the situation you or your client find yourself in? What do you know at a level of life wisdom or clinical wisdom that is relevant? This may be about yourself, your client, the wider system, the history, even things that belong in the wider world. Take a moment and mark down symbolically or with words everything that might be relevant here.

If you have used mirroring of the gesture to remove the thinking head in the previous shape it is essential to begin the fifth shape with re-placing the thinking head. This symbolic gesture is an invitation to connect with the left-brain faculty, having immersed in the more right-brain process of shape four. It marks a change of energy. In my experience the fact of having given space for the feeling dimension in shape four often frees up the capacity for more analytic or reflective thought. With the focus on analytic thought, writing the odd word in this shape can be useful, a reminder of conscious knowing or hypothesising. Returning to the first sample supervisory question above, the supervisee might mark something of their knowledge of the client's perfectionism, their critical superego and their family background where performance was all. They might also acknowledge their own personal relationship to compassion and perfectionism, the pressure they put themselves under to achieve a good outcome in the therapy, and their own lack of self-compassion in the work. In the second example the causes and contexts might be around the need for financial security, personal attitudes to change and risk, perhaps the promise or fantasy of promotion if the supervisee stays in their current role.

> Before moving to the sixth shape take a few moments to contemplate the process you have been on so far. Look through the five images you have created, the depiction of your supervisory question, your goal, the obstacle, your feelings around the situation and what you know about contributory causes and relevant contexts. When you are ready, mark in the sixth shape 'a possible next step'.

It is crucial that the sixth shape is articulated in terms of a *possibility*, rather than a *solution*. It is not "the next step" but "a next step", something, potentially small, that moves the supervisee on in the direction of attending to their supervisory concern. If it is articulated in this way there is less pressure on the supervisee to perform, either for themselves or the supervisor and therefore a higher likelihood of a creative response to the invitation.

> When you are ready, talk me through your images and what went on for you as you made them.

Figure 8.2 Reflecting on the six shapes

Once the 6S has been completed the supervisee is invited to talk through the images in sequence. If they have been working on the floor or at a table invite them firstly to come back to the dialogical setting. The role of the supervisor here is primarily to listen, but also to hold the supervisory question in mind and where appropriate to add input from the supervisory role of consultant or teacher as appropriate.

Using 6S in Group Supervision Settings

The method lends itself well to group supervision, as one of the methods that all participants can engage in simultaneously. In terms of the 'slicing of the cake' metaphor, this is a method where all get an equal slice and at the same time. The supervisor is responsible for the pacing of each shape, so that the group can start their mark-making together and end together. In a larger group it is helpful to give a time reminder – "two more minutes to complete this shape". The task of the supervisor in a group supervision session involves identifying the supervisory focus or question for each individual in the group prior to starting the technique and making a note of each of these. The supervisor helps with the articulation of the first shape in particular, according to the different enquiries. If the mark-making for the first shape is appropriate to the question the rest of the technique tends to follow quite simply. It is a powerful and tangible experience for a group to be in a non-verbal immersive process of mark-making together.

At the end of the mark-making process for the 6S there is the option for breaking into groups of two or three for the first phase of talking through the process. In a smaller group there is more time for each person to present their 6S journey to the rest of the small group. In both approaches the energy of talking after a period of quiet mark-making is a powerful contrast. In either case it is important to come back to the group as a whole for the final reflective round, to revisit the initial supervisory questions and to hear what potential 'next steps' each person identified or what they are leaving with.

As with all paper-based work the made object belongs to the maker, in this case the supervisees. From the role of supervisor as administrator it is important to clarify this explicitly so participants can decide whether to take their image with them, leave it with the supervisor or otherwise dispose of it. The supervisor may negotiate taking a photo for their supervision records.

Combining 6S with Movement Exploration

An effective variation of the method, particularly in group work, is to introduce a guided movement exploration between the mark-making phase and the discussion phase of the process.

Clear the space of art-making materials and ask the supervisees to place their sheets of paper somewhere they can see them, at the side of the room or on the wall. The supervisor then directs the supervisees to choose any of the shapes to reflect on and allow the body to move in response to that shape. There is no right or wrong way of doing this, and the presence of other group members moving can help those who might otherwise feel inhibited with this kind of exploration. The purpose is not to demonstrate the material in a performative way, but to feel it in a holistic and embodied way. After a little while the supervisor can invite the group to expand or exaggerate the movements and also to allow the voice to come through. This is a kind of crescendo of the physical exploration and is followed by a reduction or diminuendo of the process, until it becomes quiet, and the movement very small. The movement process can be repeated once or twice with other shapes from the 6S before moving into the verbal part of the reflection.

The supervisor bears in mind the time frame of the session and the size of the group when deciding whether or not to include this movement exploration. 6S works well on its own, but for some supervisees the opportunity to bring the work into the body adds depth, integration and further insights.

Using 6S in Online Supervision

The method can be adapted for online supervision. It is dependent on the supervisee having paper and art materials to hand, and enough space to comfortably mark-make during the session. The supervisee might need to move away from the computer to the floor or clear the space at their desk for the creative action part of the session. The supervisor and supervisee will need to negotiate the positioning of the camera during the mark-making. My own preference is to be able to see the supervisee rather than the sheet of paper while they are working, so I can notice the pace and feel the moment before moving on to the next shape.

After the completion of the mark-making it is helpful for the supervisor to see the image as it is being talked through. The supervisee can hold it up to the camera prior to talking through each shape or send a photo across to the supervisor.

The online Whiteboard might be a possibility for some supervisees, if they are comfortable and proficient with the use of this technology. In my own experience, most supervisees find using paper and concrete art-making materials more immersive. The Whiteboard facility seems to lend itself more to working cognitively, for example, mapping out systems or plans.

Note

1 Some of this chapter (from the start to the section on 'Facilitation of the method') is an amended and updated version of material from *Creative Supervision across Modalities: Theory and applications for therapists, counsellors and other helping professionals*, edited by Anna Chesner and Lia Zografou, Copyright © Jessica Kingsley Publishers 2014, reproduced with permission of the Licensor through PLSclear.

References

Chesner, A., and Zografou, L., eds., 2014. *Creative Supervision across Modalities.* Jessica Kingsley Publications.

de Shazer, S., 1988. *Clues: Investigating Solutions in Brief Therapy.* W. W. Norton.

Chapter 9

The Seven Step Relationship Sequence

Bryn Jones

Figure 9.0

The aim of basketball is to drop a ball through a hoop. In working or whittling wood, the aim is to transform an otherwise unremarkable piece of wood into a functional form or something which pleases the eye. In practising supervision, the aim is to gain a clear apprehension of a set of circumstances, to see things clearly. Of these three tasks, the last may well be considered to be the most challenging. Such is the complexity involved and the obstacles which stand in the way of achieving it.

As in everyday life, seeing things clearly, be it in professional or clinical settings, requires application, awareness and perseverance. The ability to settle the mind on a focal point amidst a sea of seemingly infinite demands and distractions is rare. To be able to hold it there in order that a greater and contextualised clarity might be achieved is rarer still. And finally, to sustain that focus so that the situation can be considered anew, changed and transformed through the power of seeing is rarest of all. This is the challenge of the supervisory endeavour. In reaching for such outcomes, other obstacles arise for the supervisor and their supervisee – not least our very human tendency to devise ever more complex 'solutions' to meet the seemingly complex challenges we face. We complicate complexity.

This supervisory technique attempts to counter such tendencies by providing a modest and pared down set of elements held within a deceptively simple sequential frame. This is of note, as the technique's principal field of enquiry is that most

DOI: 10.4324/9781003435655-12

complex supervisory terrain: the third and fourth supervisory Eyes (Hawkins and Mahon, 2020) concerned with human relationships (see Chapter 3).

- Eye Three – the therapeutic or working relationship, in particular the transference aspects in terms of how the client may be experiencing the therapist or coach
- Eye Four – the therapeutic or working relationship, in particular the countertransference aspect in terms of the therapist's or coach's experience in relation to the client, the client's system and the material of the work

The Seven Step Relationship Sequence (7SRS) was first trialled, honed and developed as part of the London Centre for Psychodrama's Creative Approaches to Supervision in 2018. In 2020 it became one of the professionally field-tested and validated techniques that form the core of the training's action method portfolio.

I have had a long-standing interest in reflective, contemplative practice and have been a practitioner of meditation since 1989. Over the years, such practice has guided, supported and informed my interest and subsequent career in psychology, psychotherapy and supervision. I mention this here, as this supervisory technique draws on particular aspects of meditation practice often referred to as 'attention shifting' or 'attention switching'. It is of note that several other techniques taught on the Creative Supervision Training incorporate similar 'perspective shifting' characteristics: Small World (Chapter 4), Role Work (Chapter 5), Cycle of Change (Chapter 7) and the Framework for the Embodied Reflective Narrative (Chapter 11).

In classical meditation and mindfulness, this approach involves the practitioner shifting their attention from one point of focus to another. For example, from a general awareness of one's body to a particular sensation within the body, such as the sensation of breathing. Building pathways towards deeper and more penetrating meditative states such as samatha-vipassanā (tranquil insight) the practice enables the practitioner to develop a quality of cognitive flexibility, a mental suppleness. This in turn allows them to cultivate a broader, integrated and more comprehensive perspective on a particular situation or, in the case of this supervisory application, the practitioner–client/other relationship.

This is especially helpful as for many, when in relational contact with another, there tends to be a narrowing in perspective. The 7SRS technique provides the practitioner with a stable and differentiated position which prevents the field of attention from collapsing. 7SRS supports and sustains a contextualised outlook and overview from which important ambient and peripheral information may be noticed and considered.

In her 2022 article for the Zeitschrift für Psychodrama und Soziometrie *Tele, Transference and Countertransference in Supervision* (2022), Chesner discusses the 7SRS in relation to the psychodramatic concept of Tele. Readers interested in expanding their understanding of the 7SRS method will find that article helpful as a complementary and insightful commentary to what I set out here.

Chesner discusses how "the Morenian idea of Tele enriches our understanding of what happens between people" (Chesner, 2022: 3). This speaks to the very heart of this method in that it examines the relational dynamic that occurs when two people meet, work and grow *together* in therapy and coaching spaces. It recognises that the relationship between practitioner and client is affectual and that it involves exchange and change for both parties. The 7SRS looks to acknowledge, track and measure the insight described by Carl Jung as "The meeting of two personalities (being) like contact between two chemical substances: if there is any reaction, both are transformed" (Jung, 1955: 49).

In the 7SRS there is a switching of supervisory attention between two relational perspectives: that of the practitioner and that of the client. In tracking an oscillation between these two points of view, the practitioner is able to maintain or return to a position of differentiation in relation to the client/other. Here the method can be helpful in instances of enmeshment or over-identification on the side of the practitioner. Invariably from time to time, we all work with individuals with whom we have shared generational, cultural or lived experiences. There can be a risk that the practitioner associates or 'leans in' too much and so the necessary distance for context and insight blurs or is lost. Equally the method supports awareness where a practitioner is reacting away from a client/other and adopting a polarised or split position. The method provides a reliable counterbalance for either tendency. In supervision, with the aid of this method, the practitioner can get sight of such dynamics to clarify and reset their position accordingly.

It is through this process of attention shifting that an illuminating insight is achieved. The method provides three perspectives. The supervisee puts themselves in the shoes of the other to see themselves through the other's eyes. They then return to their own position, as it is imagined by the other, to see the other afresh from this unique and differentiated perspective. Finally, as the 7SRS is a projective method, they are able to consider this interplay from a third perspective and so formulate their own supervision of the relationship under examination.

Mentalisation and Imagination

There are apparent links here between the 7SRS, the concept of mentalisation and the key role of the imagination. Mentalisation describes the effort an individual makes to understand the thoughts, feelings, beliefs and opinions of themselves and others. It is at the heart of sense-making and meaning-making.

> When we mentalise we are engaged in a form of (mostly preconscious) imaginative activity that enables us to perceive and interpret human behaviour in terms of intentional mental states (e.g., needs, desires, feelings, beliefs, goal, purposes and reasons). Mentalizing must be imaginative because we have to imagine what other people might be thinking or feeling.
>
> (Fonagy and Allison, 2012: 12)

In the 7SRS method's use of image cards, there is another purposeful invitation towards the imaginative. This signals a move away from left hemispherical dominance, which might seek answers and understanding from a purely rational and logical perspective. The technique supports the practitioner towards a more right-inclined hemispherical perspective. Intuitive and metaphorical insights are accessed which can bring startlingly new, rich and valuable takes on the relationship under examination.

These imaginal enquiries are cohered within the linearity and simplicity of the 7SRS frame. This acts as a clear container which holds and facilitates the back-and-forth, alternating rhythm of the technique. This allows the supervisee to visit and transition between the two alternating points of view, their own as practitioner and that of their client. Here again we see the mechanics of mentalisation appearing as an integrated part of the technique.

As the supervisee's attention refines, they may experience a kind of 'dropping down' into a state of absorption. This quality has been described by dramatherapist pioneer Peter Slade in his seminal work *Child Drama* as, "being completely wrapped up in what is being done or what one is doing, to the exclusion of all other thoughts, including the awareness of or desire for an audience. A strong form of concentration" (Slade, 1954: 32).

This absorbed way of being enables the supervisee to move fluidly between conscious and less conscious forms of insight and knowing, thus enriching and adding texture to the relationship under their consideration. It is as if they have entered a playful and highly sophisticated perceptive dance around the focus of their enquiry. Through this they are able to construct a multidimensional picture of the relationship. Mentalisation and imagination, conscious and unconscious attention and perception coalesce to create a finely detailed and comprehensive MRI-like mental image of the relationship as a whole:

> We have come to conceive of mentalisation as a multidimensional construct, whose core processing dimensions are underpinned by distinct neural systems. Thus mentalisation involves both a self-reflective and interpersonal component; it is based both on observing others and reflecting on their mental states, it is both implicit and explicit and concerns both feelings and cognitions.
>
> (Fonagy and Allison, 2012: 16)

Focusing the Inquiry and Honing the Supervisory Question

As mentioned above, the 7SRS technique has a specific and focused relevance to those supervisory questions which engage the third and/or the fourth of the supervisory Eyes, the client/practitioner relationship and the practitioner's process. It will not be an effective method to use in relation to the other Eyes. Its domain is that of the relational, to support enquiries around what is going on between practitioner and client. What is the client/other seeking or needing and how are they presenting themselves in the relationship? How might they be experiencing the practitioner and what feelings, expectations, hopes or fears might they be holding in relation to them? Similarly, the technique will support a practitioner to gain insight into their own countertransferential experiences to notice how and why they find themselves reacting in a particular way to a client/other or the material they bring to supervision.

These apparent limitations in the technique's scope are also its strength, reflecting again its clear and uncomplicated quality. When employed for its specific purpose (i.e. to serve Eye Three and Eye Four), the 7SRS can often provide clear and illuminating insights through otherwise complex and convoluted narratives.

Facilitating the Supervisory Method

To facilitate this method, you will need a piece of cloth which can be folded into an oblong shape of approximately 60 cm × 20 cm and a selection of image cards. These can be a variety of postcards or a pack of metaphoric cards. One observation regarding the choice of cards is to avoid using those which have specifically attributed qualities assigned to them, such as archetype cards. It is helpful to the process of the method that the images used hold no definitive meaning, so they can be selected according to the inclinations, interpretations and needs of the supervisee.

Once the supervisory question is sufficiently honed, look to identify a working space, either on the floor or a tabletop. Offer the supervisee the cloth and ask them to fold it into an oblong shape, similar to the shape of a letterbox so that it sits horizontally in the space before them. This provides the frame within which the image cards will be placed to create the 7SRS.

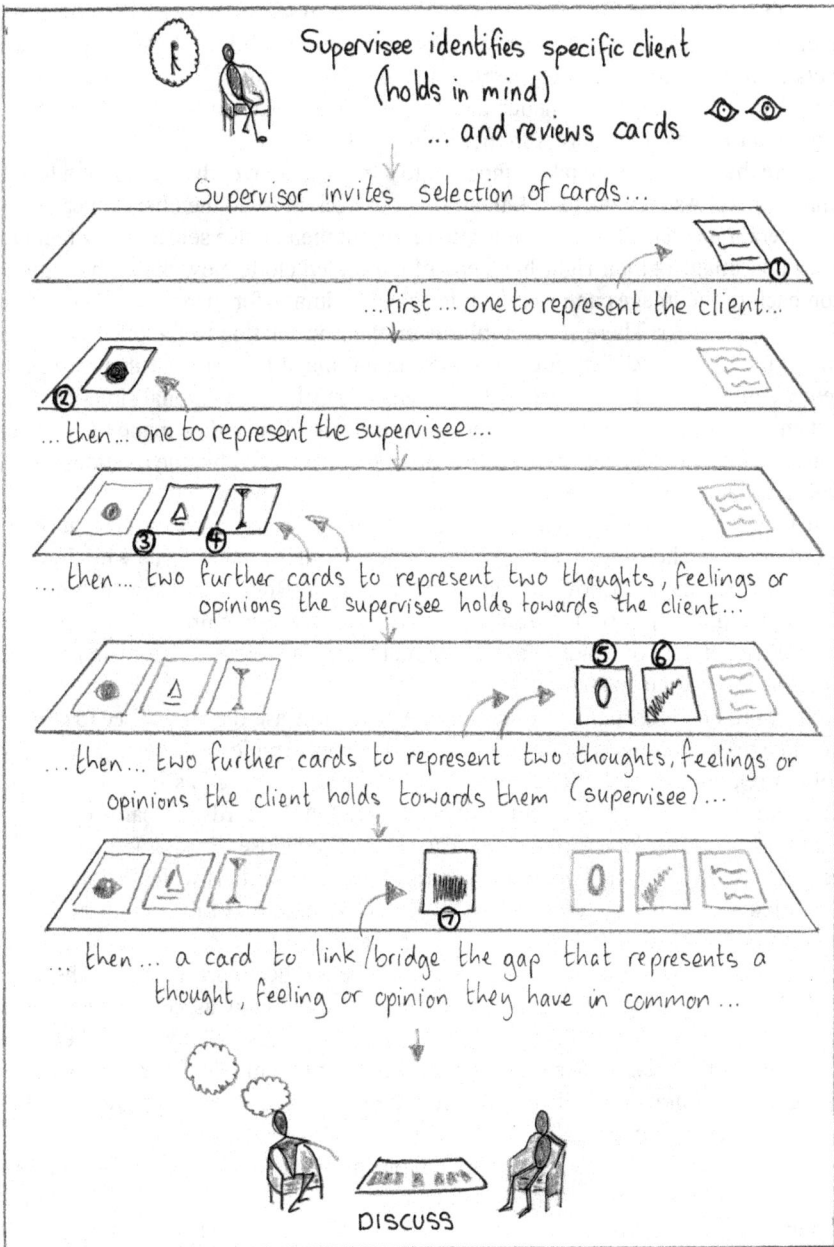

Figure 9.1 The Seven Step Relationship Sequence

As the supervisee folds and arranges the cloth/frame, the supervisor places a selection of approximately twenty cards higgledy-piggledy on the floor/surface (outside of the frame). Through arranging them in this looser, randomised manner, there is a call to the spontaneous and the intuitive, particularly helpful for those who tend to locate themselves in their thinking function.

Invite the supervisee to take a moment to simply look over the images and to see what is there. As they do so, ask them to bring back to mind the client/other under consideration and to choose an image to represent them. Once selected, ask them to place that image at their right-hand end of the folded cloth. Now direct their attention back to the images and ask them to select an image for themselves *in relation* to this client/other. There is an emphasis on them in relation to the other which is important to convey. They are not choosing an image to represent themselves in general but one to reflect how they turn up in this particular relational situation. Say just enough to give them a clear steer in this direction. Once they make their selection, ask them to place this card, representing themselves within the relationship, at their left-hand end of the cloth.

It is worth mentioning that there is no discussion being initiated here, just the act of intuitive choosing. The supervisor is not asking the supervisee why they are choosing the images or how they are feeling about it. Brevity and succinctness are key, so as to avoid intruding upon the supervisee's intuitive process. Allow them an uninterrupted space to drop down and feel their way towards receiving prompts from the side of the images.

The third and fourth image selections are next. Now ask the supervisee to choose two images which represent two thoughts, feelings, opinions or beliefs that they hold in relation to their client. Once selected these are placed as if to form a line from the card representing themselves and stretching towards the card representing the client, from their left to right. They are placed close to the practitioner card because although they are about the client they are perceptions which belong to the practitioner. In this way, they invariably reflect something of the countertransference and tele elements which are alive in the relationship.

The focus now shifts back to that of the client/other represented by the card positioned on the opposite right-hand end of the cloth. Now ask the supervisee to choose two images which represent two thoughts, feelings, opinions or beliefs that they *believe* the client/other may hold in relation to them. Here the supervisee is being asked to draw on their imagination, their intuitive knowledge and their felt sense of what their client/other *might* be making of them.

The apparent ambiguity of this invitation might raise challenges for some as they venture into a creative and imaginal process. In such instances, a creative supervisor able to naturally model belief in both the approach and the method will reassure the supervisee and sustain them in accomplishing this step in the inquiry.

Once selected, these two images are placed to mirror the previous pattern, this time forming a line from the card representing the client/other towards the card representing the practitioner from right to left. These are placed close to the client/

other card because they represent the client's/other's view of the practitioner as imagined by the practitioner.

So, at this stage six cards have been chosen and placed – on the left side three images associated with the practitioner and on the right three images associated with the client/other. A space remains in the middle, between these two sequences of three cards. This space is for the seventh and final card.

Now ask your supervisee to choose an image that reflects something that is true for both themselves as practitioner and their client; a thought, feeling or opinion that they share or hold in relation to one another. This image, once selected and placed, functions as a kind of bridging card linking the two individuals and their impressions of one another and completing the 7SRS.

At this point, the supervisor gathers up the remaining, unused image cards and puts them to one side. By removing the surplus image cards, the 7SRS as represented by the seven selected images becomes the sole focus of attention. Invite the supervisee to take stock and view the sequence in its entirety. At this point new aspects might come to light as hitherto unseen or unintended narratives and connections emerge from the interplay of the cards set in their particular sequence. Similarly, a supervisee might suddenly notice specific or recurring elements which add new depth or resonance to what was being considered in their selection process.

It is of course also possible that a supervisee simply sees what they have selected in more prosaic and matter-of-fact ways. This might indicate the clarity and acuity of the selections they have made or reflect something of their way of working. Nevertheless, taking a moment to notice, acknowledge and digest the overall sequence is usually of help. It also marks a point of transition whereby the supervisee returns from the relatively solitary creative absorption of curating the images to come back to the live dyad of the supervisory relationship.

Now ask the supervisee what was behind their choosing. Invite them to talk through and describe the cards laid out in the frame. I have found it helpful to follow the order in which they were chosen. This feels clear and containing, as if following a sequence of markers that have previously been laid. This part of the process has a quality of *show and tell*. As the supervisee performs this role, another layer of new and emergent elements may appear – associated thoughts and feelings, reminders of aspects of the work to date and other peripheral material. These may support deeper insights and/or relate back in significant ways to the original supervisory question. In any case, this step provides a dialogic space whereby supervisee and supervisor review together with interest and curiosity, the cards that have been selected, their connections and their possible meanings.

Finally, taking their cue from the time boundary of the session or a salient point to pause, the supervisor signals a conclusion to the process. Invite the supervisee to derole the images and return them to the original pack of cards and to derole the cloth and place it to the side. Supervisor and supervisee return to their original seats, echoing how they were seated at the beginning of the session. Having now returned to the conscious supervisor–supervisee relational space, the supervisor recalls for the supervisee the original supervisory question. Time can be spent reflecting on what relevant responses may have been offered up by the creative method in answer to this question. If relevant or needed, a final consideration around '*what is being taken away*' can provide a fitting and coherent end.

Concluding Considerations and Reflections

Having now taught this method on the course and developed it within my own practice for over several years, there are a number of considerations and reflections that it may be helpful to share. These reflect some frequently asked questions and helpful clarifications which have arisen through teaching and practice.

Expansive insight: Although the 7SRS method can provide very clear and specific solutions to challenging relational dilemmas, it seems important to note that it is not a solution-focused method. The key strengths of the method lie in how it supports a supervisee to develop skill and competency in forming a richer, nuanced and multidimensional awareness of the dynamics at play within a particular relationship. Through practising the method, the supervisee can develop their acuity in noticing, reflecting and connecting otherwise disparate elements. This enables a progressive insight and awareness to naturally emerge as a key competency. Simultaneously, the supervisee familiarises themselves with the meditation/mindfulness skill I mention above, *attention shifting*. This also is a practical skill that can be gradually integrated to enrich and refine other areas of relational practice be that in clinical, supervisory, teaching or coaching contexts.

Non-interpretive: This is not a method where supervisor or supervisee are looking to interpret the images in pursuit of identifying their supposed absolute or inherent meaning. Rather, it is an explorative and imaginative process that provides new, revelatory and otherwise unconsidered insights. The role of the supervisor in facilitating this method is to direct the method with clarity, following the prescribed sequence and being mindful to language the invitations in ways which support the supervisee's open and intuitive curiosity.

No coincidences: As with all projective processes, I am increasingly minded to believe there are no coincidences in such imaginative and creative work. This means that when creating art, building stories and narratives, etc., the seemingly random or chance occurrences are often not truly coincidental, but rather the result of the practitioner's subconscious mind drawing upon experiences, influences and patterns they have absorbed. This can lead to a seemingly 'coincidental' connection surfacing from within the work but one that rings astonishingly true with insight, depth and meaning.

Acceptance: The above is greatly aided by facilitating the method in a spirit of acceptance. For example, the supervisee not liking the images is okay. As supervisor–facilitator of the method, support your supervisee to accept and be with the images as they are. As above, the supervisee's initial feelings about the images or the prospect of the method need not be positive. If allowed, the images and the process they delineate will do their work in time. Indeed, their not being immediately liked by the supervisee may be an important part of the story about to be told. Similarly, be alert and curious around any unbidden communications that are prompted by the cards, especially those that are not part of a supervisee's conscious story. Be ready to support supervisees who may be prone to overthink or hold perfectionist-like traits. Help them to slow down and drop into a more immersive and less rational process. In this, the subtle skill of the supervisor is required. Look to open up the imaginative field, not through forcing or overdirecting but by suggestions, prompts and nudges. It is a subtle and nuanced process. Patience may be required. Help the supervisee to relax and gradually give themselves over to the images. Careful and discerning language can be especially helpful here. You may encourage your supervisee by reflecting, "Looks like this is a complex and multi-layered situation we're exploring. It may take us some time to get the clarity we seek. Let the images help you towards achieving that." This notion, that when working creatively, the materials being worked with shape and contribute to the process, is a familiar one to the artist or creative practitioner.

Trust and belief: Occasionally you may work with a supervisee who is unfamiliar with creative approaches and/or sceptical and resistant to the more open explorations and associations they invite. In this, the supervisor may need to model a trust in the individual's creative capacity and a belief that the method can usefully serve them. A sensitively articulated communication of trust in the supervisee enables them to at least 'give the method a go'. This can be a difficult task for the supervisor but one worth leaning into. The results can be profoundly transformative, as the supervisee not only finds the method useful but also discovers a significant perceptual shift which they can carry across to other areas of their life and practice. To support themselves in this endeavour, the facilitating supervisor can be helped by familiarising themselves with the varying roles of the supervisor (Chapter 3) and skilfully selecting an optimum approach.

As with all projective methods an appreciation of aesthetic distance serves the efficacy of the approach well. Be alert to supervisees who seek to identify a hard, literal meaning from the chosen images. Guide them to work more receptively, to be open and curious around what the image suggests, evokes or reflects rather than what it might mean in any absolute way. Joseph Campbell would call this "not damaging the image" and that when working creatively with such myths and images that they are "to be read, therefore, not literally, but as metaphors" (Campbell, 2002: p. 28).

Online applications: The 7SRS is a method that can transfer very successfully for online applications. In facilitating this method online, the following recommendations will help preserve some of the special characteristics which are a natural part of the in-person experience.

Firstly, some prior planning is required. Ensure your supervisee attends the session with their own physical set of image cards and a cloth for the stage/frame. The three-dimensional and tactile nature of handling and folding the cloth and the choosing, placing, moving and sequencing of the images in real time is an important part of the process. Using electronic on-screen images is not recommended. This flattens out the overall experience and the more embodied elements of being in direct contact with material elements are lost.

Guide your supervisee towards an 'as close as possible' approximation of the in-person method. Direct them to create the cloth frame and to then set out the image cards. Hold the space for them to take in the images and then guide them in the method. It is preferable for you to be able to view the creation of the sequence within the frame as they work. If they have two cameras or are able to tilt the direction of their camera, this is ideal. If not, support them to make the selections and create the sequence first, based on your direction.

Once all images have been selected and arranged in sequence, remember to direct them to clear away the unused cards. This achieves a hygiene and clarity whereby the seven cards selected sit and can be seen clearly within the frame. The supervisee can then briefly lift and show the image they are referring to. Again, this will follow the same order as above, as they describe what was behind their choice of each image in turn.

Towards the end of the process, be attentive to support them in deroling the images, clearing away the materials and setting them to one side. In this you are providing an approximation of them 'returning to their original seat', that of the conscious practitioner. Once there, you can begin the reflective and conclusion round, revisiting the supervisory question and, if required, a consideration of next steps.

Eye Eight: In the writing of this chapter, I have found myself thinking about how the method relates to Eye Eight. I had not considered this before. I am not suggesting the method be used to explicitly explore Eye Eight issues but more to note that it does offer a clear mirror in which a useful reflection of the practitioner self might appear and be considered. The spirit of the method echoes that of the supervisory endeavour, a wholly relational prospect which works best when it is most truly collaborative. I am referring here to those occasions when supervisor and supervisee, regardless of their respective experience levels, share the enquiry together. This sees them working in a form of relational exchange that shifts between varying perspectives to elucidate and clarify an otherwise vague notion. In this, the task for the supervisor is to identify the place whereby they might most usefully step onto this shared pathway of emergent knowledge and journey *with* their supervisee towards insight. In doing so, both our supervisee and ourselves as supervisor may come to see more clearly the kind of practitioner we are or might become.

References

Campbell, J., 2002. *The Inner Reaches of Outer Space: Metaphor as Myth and as Religion.* Harper and Row.

Chesner, A., 2022. "Tele, Transference and Countertransference". In *Zeitschrift für Psychodrama und Soziometrie, 21*(2), 97–104. https://doi.org/10.1007/s11620-022-00699-0. Accessed 11 September 2024.

Chesner, A., and Zografou, L., eds., 2014. *Creative Supervision across Modalities.* Jessica Kingsley Publications.

Fonagy, P., and Allison, E., 2012. "What Is Mentalization". In Midgley, N., and Vrouva, I., eds.. *Minding the Child, Mentalization-based interventions with Children, Young People and their Families.* Routledge.

Hawkins, P., and McMahon, A., 2020. *Supervision in the Helping Professions.* Open University Press.

Jung, C., 1955. *Modern Man in Search of a Soul.* Mariner.

Osbon, D.K., ed., 1991. *Reflections on the Art of Living.* Harper Collins.

Slade, P., 1954. *Child Drama.* University of London Press.

Chapter 10

Mandala

Bryn Jones

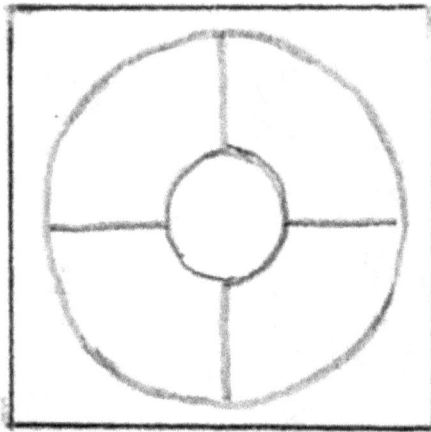

Figure 10.0

Background

Supervisory practice involving the use of mandala motifs has appeared in this training since its inception in the 1990s. The technique, as originally described by Sue Jennings (Jennings, 1997), has continued to be taught as part of the LCP supervision training. In recent years, however, the basic frame of this has evolved and developed to incorporate new perspectives, including Anna Chesner's innovation of a more articulated embodied dimension. The addition of an embodied aspect to mandala practice has also been explored by Nisha Sajnani who describes how this enables individuals to "experience issues in the 'here and now' and serves the more pragmatic function of preparing them for conscious reflection" (Sajnani, 2002: 14). In outlining the method as it is currently taught on the course, there is an acknowledgement of both the legacy of the original technique, its more recent developments and its continuing importance as a key creative method on the LCP Creative Supervision Training.

DOI: 10.4324/9781003435655-13

It seems that when we think and speak of life, we frequently think of it as being circular. We talk of life cycles, the circle of life and so forth. This cyclical nature, especially when considered developmentally, echoes something of the rhythm of the seasons. Those markers of time that appear in the natural world and that come around again and again and again. Against these we measure our own journeys, birth, ageing, sickness and death; rising and falling, inhaling and exhaling; and growing, living, waning and dying.

There is a link here between the mandala method described below and another discrete technique taught on the course entitled *Cycle of Change*. This is based on Liz White's *Seasons of Change* (White, 2002) and Ann Hale's *Sociometric Cycle* (Hale cited in White, 2002: 94). It has been adapted as a valuable action-based method and is facilitated for the students as they approach the completion of their training and the conclusion of the course. See Chapter 7 for more on this particular approach and technique.

Roundness

Towards the end of his seminal work *The Poetics of Space* (Bachelard, 1994) the philosopher and architect Gaston Bachelard turns his attention to reflect on the nature of our (human) being through the varying lenses of phenomenology, ontology and metapsychology. Through these he identifies and links what he describes as several 'primitive' truths. That is to say, truths that are not expressed for astonishing effect, nor are linguistically clumsy but which provide a clear and immediate meaning through plain and direct language; "They appear and in a twinkling they are completed" (Bachelard, 1994: 233). These include the philosopher Karl Jaspers's comment that "Every being seems in itself round" (Jaspers, 1947: 50); the artist Vincent van Gogh's notion that "Life is probably round" (van Gogh, 1882: 249); and the poet Joë Bousquet who wrote, "He had been told that life was beautiful. No! Life is round!" (Bousquet, 1989: 174). All concur on this characteristic roundness to our ways of being. To Bachelard, these truths indicate the essential roundness of ourselves, the lives we create and inhabit. And, appearing in the final few pages of his book, he sounds his plaintive call to realise such truths and "gather our being into its centre" (Bachelard, 1994: 234). In this he reflects the essential aim of the mandala.

Mandala is a Sanskrit word meaning circle. Its defining aesthetic is now most commonly recognised by an increasingly familiar visual motif. This comprises a geometric configuration of an outer circle which contains four quadrants with a smaller circle at its centre. This image comes to us today via ancient Hindu–Buddhist meditational traditions. It represents a cosmic sacred space and provides a focus for the meditational and/or devotional practices of an adept. In this the mandala represents an idealised universe through which the adept 'travels', accumulating insight and realisation as they progress. In arriving at the 'heart' of the mandala, a sacred unity with the mandala deity or the realisation they symbolise is achieved. The mandala then is both a physical diagram to guide spiritual practice and a visualised manifestation of that particular spiritual realisation.

When we employ Mandala in a supervisory context we draw on some of these elements in order to support the supervisee in their own creative and imaginative process. The method facilitates a reflective journey through varying points of view. The process aids insight by identifying otherwise disparate aspects of the supervisee's way of being. This is reflected within the mandala as an integrated vision, one which encompasses both the personal and the professional and is held in relation to their sense of core values or essential purpose.

The opportunity afforded by this practice to observe from varying points of view is a key aspect of mandala practice. The journey is not linear but one of circumambulation around a central point. The continuity of this process transcends the limitations of a journey which travels from here to there, from a beginning to an end and which is then left forgotten within one's wake. This journey is recurrent, evolving and accumulative. It is as if in arriving, dwelling and reflecting within one quadrant, the others are recast and renewed in meaning. This is especially so if taken up as a regular practice which I will discuss later.

In supervision the invitation to the supervisee is to become present and attentive to their emerging and authentic practitioner self. The focus of such supervisory enquiry supports the supervisee to pause and take stock of where they are at this particular juncture in their practice. In this regard the method provides an especially useful frame for the consideration of Eye Eight, responding to the inquiry around personal and professional identity. See Chapter 3 for more on this newly articulated supervisory eye.

This paper-based mandala technique enables the supervisee to recall and gather past salient experience whilst simultaneously being alive to new material and insights that surface through the creation of the mandala itself. It is an essential and dynamic interplay, whereby a synthesis of 'what was' combines with 'what is' to create a rich, compelling and immediate appreciation of the present. This is a key attribute of mandala practice as a tool towards integrative insight. It provides what Carl Jung describes as,

> Formation, transformation and eternal recreation ... where all the paths I had been following, all the steps I had taken, were leading back to a single point – namely, to the midpoint. It became increasingly plain to me that the mandala is the centre, the exponent of all paths.
>
> (Jung, 1989: 196)

I will now set out the essential sequential steps for both the embodied and paper-based versions of the method. I will also add some accompanying commentary to guide and support its facilitation.

Focusing the Enquiry and Honing the Supervisory Question

The method is an excellent tool to use as part of a review of practice or other Eye Eight-related considerations. The supervisee might ask themselves, "Where am I as a practitioner? What supports, sustains and develops my practice? What might be stalling or inhibiting my fuller development?" These reflections serve as sufficient material for the supervisory question.

As with all mandala practice, the method provides a clearly defined mirror in which the supervisee can see reflected back their personal preferences, choices and actions. What appears clearly in the mirror can then be thought about and discussed more generally. The Mandala method may be of particular use to a supervisee who finds themselves being carried along by a recurrent stream of external demands. Similarly, a practitioner who appears especially focused on accomplishing goals may discover hitherto unseen resources, new insights around blind spots and the possibility of a caring and compassionate take on the consequences of endless striving. There is within this technique a real and tangible acknowledgement of the practitioner self – a coming back to source in ways which are affirming, self-caring and grounding. We are not only practitioners, we are people.

The method as it is taught on the training comprises two key phases. The first is embodied and the second employs a projective mark-making technique. These two can be used in unison or singularly depending on the supervisee's interests and needs, limitations of time and the setting and context of the supervision session.

Facilitating the Supervisory Method

Embodied Warmup

Beginning with an embodied element, there is the recognition of this method as encompassing an integrated mind/body approach, that is, one which seeks to engage and combine the multifarious constituent dimensions that characterise a person. This then accords with the form and function of the mandala as being a symbolic unifying process towards actualising wholeness.

The embodied element also reflects the dynamic nature of a mandala. There is a tendency to view images and motifs as if they are static. The actual mandala process however holds an underlying sense of movement.

Invite your supervisee to move freely and orientate themselves within the space. As they do so, guide them to notice and connect with their physical being, spatial orientation, sensations, the quality of their breathing etc.

Guide them to choose a place to pause and to stand in that chosen place. Give them time to settle into a comfortable and grounded stance in stillness. Ask them to place their attention in the centre of the body, the central point from which movement can happen. As they do so, ask them to connect to the personal and professional *core beliefs and values* that they hold. Take a moment to connect with and deepen these recognitions. In this your supervisee is coming into presence by holding these key individual elements that will be represented at the centre of the mandala.

Now guide them to reach up with their left hand as if taking apples from an over-hanging branch. As they do so, invite them to connect with those sources of *guidance, inspiration and encouragement* that support, sustain and enrich their practice, bringing to mind the people, places and things that guide and inspire them. These might appear in the form of teachers, role models, theorists and theories, practition-ers, philosophers, artists etc. It may include special places, artworks, phrases and individuals living or deceased, who in some way function to guide, inspire, sustain and progress them in their practice. Once sufficient time has been given to identify and form such connections, they lower their hand.

Next, in a similar way, guide your supervisee to reach upwards or outwards with their right hand. Here they are reaching to identify and connect with personal *skills, strengths and competencies* which have been cultivated and are ready to be offered to others.

After some time identifying and acknowledging these accomplishments within their own experience, invite them to use and move their right foot and leg to connect with notions of uncertainty, of being off balance. Here there is contact with those less developed practitioner qualities, *anxieties, vulnerabilities and weaknesses.* In this the supervisee is connecting with their *inner client.* Similarly, there is time to notice and to be with these, to acknowledge them as currently appearing but in ways which avoid self-blame or shame. In this way they are in touch with aspects of their practice that may benefit from further care and attention going forwards.

The momentum of this moving enquiry now transfers across the body to animate the left leg and foot. This is now moved in an exploratory way to connect with creativity. It is as if the body touches a pool of creative potential. This draws and supports reflection upon *the role of creativity in your practice and your life.* Again, time is provided to consider this, to notice and be curious about how and what is discovered through this point of attention and turn of gesture.

Invite your supervisee to find their way to bring their movement explorations to a close. Here there is a moment to acknowledge these dimensions together, as aspects of self, gathered, present and interconnected.

Mark-making Approach

Having connected with and warmed up to this mandala-based practice via an embodied, felt-sense activity, there is now the opportunity to explore it further on the page as a mark-making activity. This paper-based projective approach creates a type of 'aesthetic distance'. This provides the supervisee with a new perspective and one which allows for a sustained quality of stillness to support absorption and focus.

Projective methods "enable a dramatic dialogue to take place between an internally held situation ... and the external expression of that situation" (Jones, 1996: 131). Through this, the supervisee is able to "create, discover, and engage with external representations of inner conflicts" (Jones, 1996: 132). These representations can appear with spontaneous immediacy on the page, within the 'third space' of the mandala frame. Supervisee and supervisor are able to simultaneously see them as they appear on the paper. Later together they can review and consider their meaning, thereby supporting a rich, dialogic and collaborative supervisory relationship.

To begin, the supervisor provides the supervisee with a sheet of plain paper and a selection of drawing materials. The use of bold mark-making materials such as oil or chalk pastels, wax crayons and charcoal sticks can be helpful to support supervisees to work more freely and openly within a creative frame. Providing art materials that can be smudged, used freely and expressively can assist in this regard.

In using the term 'mark-making', the idea is to avoid any potentially off-putting or inhibitory notions associated with performing an 'art activity'. Artistic competency is neither necessary nor called for in this method. Some supervisees may create detailed and elaborate illustrative pieces, some will incline more towards abstract shapes and others may quite literally make a few marks on the page. All are fine. The key point is to support the supervisee to bring an open and thoughtful curiosity to what has emerged through the method. The supervisor joins them in their reflections, prompting and encouraging them to wonder anew and explore what their illustrative work represents. Gradually, it is hoped that new insights come into focus, bringing a clearer sense of both themselves as a practitioner and their practice.

Some supervisees may appear hesitant to commit such notions to paper. They may be unfamiliar with working creatively and especially so within a supervisory space, under the gaze of their supervisor. This method, along with the others described in this book, provides something of a countercultural turn to the more hierarchical orthodoxies of supervision. Here is supervision as a shared, explorative and experimental enquiry which employs creativity as both an energising fuel and a guiding and illuminating light. The supervisor is present, attentive and engaged and adopts a facilitative role, joining the supervisee in a spirit of collaborative and creative enquiry.

It is helpful for the creative supervisor to be alert to such dynamics and to work to mediate these as required. Supporting your supervisee's engagement with the creative method is the first step in the process. As the facilitating supervisor you may find it helpful to offer some examples to reassure or prompt thinking but be mindful to avoid doing the work for your supervisee.

The first task is to create a mandala motif incorporating two circles: a large outer circle which contains a smaller circle at its centre.

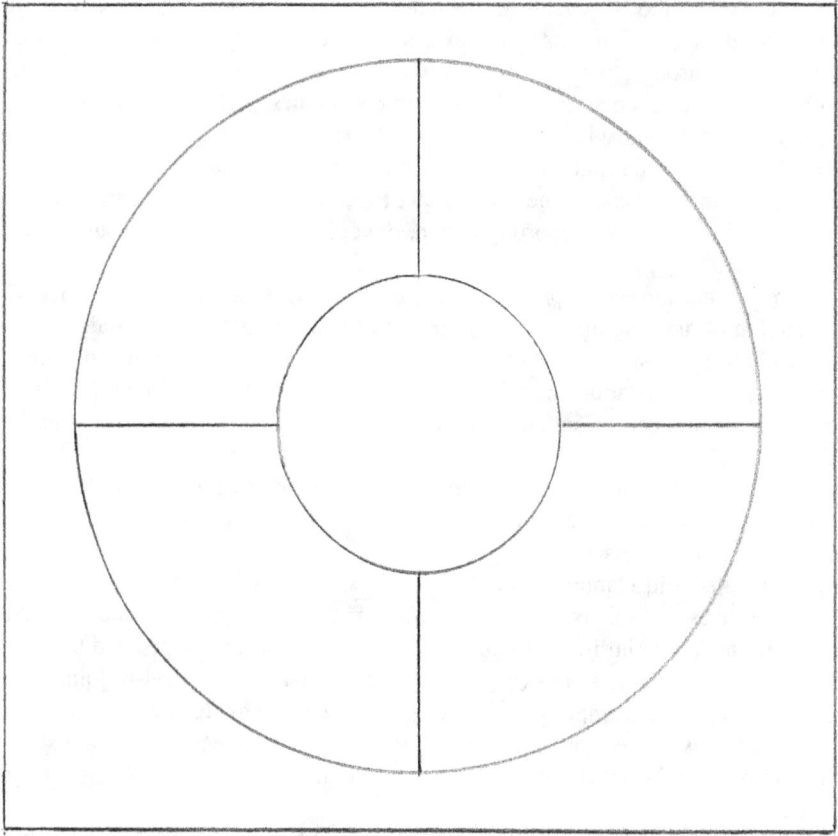

Figure 10.1 Template for Mandala

The space in between these two circles is then divided into four equal quadrants.

The supervisor facilitates the method supporting the supervisee to focus firstly on the smaller, central circle and then on each of the four quadrants in turn, following a clockwise sequence. Each location holds a particular focus as follows:

1 The inner circle – core beliefs and values.
2 The upper left quadrant – guides and inspirations.
3 The upper right quadrant – skills, strengths and competencies.
4 The lower right quadrant – anxieties, vulnerabilities and weaknesses.
5 The lower left quadrant – the role of creativity.

These then mirror the same sequence as visited in the embodied approach above. This time, however, the responses will be made via mark-making on the paper rather than through embodied physical gestures. In each area, the supervisee is invited to dwell and reflect and to make marks in ways that illustrate, capture, represent and symbolise responses and reflections to each given area of enquiry. The encouragement is to mark-make, draw and illustrate rather than to write words.

The Inner Circle: Core Beliefs and Values
The process begins by gathering attention into that which lies at the centre of this mandala. Presently this appears as a small, empty circular disc. Classically, the heart of the mandala is where the deity or that which is to be realised resides. Taking a cue from this notion, in our supervisory mandala, we invite the supervisee to identify and connect with their own underpinning beliefs and values. Those personal, perhaps private principles, that define why they practice in the way they do, and which characterise the kind of practitioner they are or aspire to become. The invitation here is to now bring these front and centre, to declare them at the outset of this evolving enquiry by placing them at the very heart of their personal mandala and to mark their intended integration with the mandala as a whole. Sometimes, the supervisee may experience a sudden and immediate sense of coherence and completion in this apparently simple act. At other times, there is a dissonance and a discrepancy. A sense of there still being some important work to be done around the alignment of personal values with their way of practising. The task here is to find a way to represent them with an illustrative form, image or symbol, within the small empty disc at the mandala's heart.

The Upper Left Quadrant – Guides and Inspirations
Alongside the creativity of the task at hand, the thinking function is very much engaged within these initial quadrants. This begins with the identification and representation of those externally sourced aspects of practice, including guidance, support, encouragement, inspiration, theoretical frameworks, modalities, respected individuals and philosophical perspectives. This can include anyone or anything that we might reach for to enrich, feed, deepen, grow and expand our practice and ourselves as a practitioner. These reflections may well prompt thinking around more specific theoretical, rational and conceptual considerations, as the practitioner reviews what is needed to supplement and strengthen themselves in achieving effective practice.

The Upper Right Quadrant – Skills, Strengths and Competencies
The next step follows a clockwise direction moving to the north-eastern quadrant. Here, ask your supervisee to bring to mind those skills, strengths and competencies which already characterise and/or underpin their clear, confident and effective practice. Guide them to identify those that they are familiar with and which they utilise regularly. This is a space for professional self-acknowledgement. The supervisee is encouraged to mark those skills and accomplishments that they now possess and which qualify them as a competent practitioner. Examples might include skill in practice-based techniques, use of reflective language, theoretical knowledge, containment and boundary maintenance. The supervisee works to identify these qualities and to then find their own way of representing them on the paper via mark-making. Once sufficient time has been held for this, the supervisor signals a move onwards.

The Lower Right Quadrant – Anxieties, Vulnerabilities and Weaknesses

Continuing to follow the clockwise course, the supervisee's attention now settles within the south-eastern quadrant. This quadrant invites the identification of that which is underdeveloped in their practice. This might include aspects of practice that bring anxiety and that feel in need of further resourcing, development or integration. This is a tender enquiry. It is helpful if the supervisor can be alive to this and modulate their facilitation accordingly. In closely tracking the supervisees' process, the supervisor works sensitively to help their supervisee *lean into* these developing edges of their practice. This is important in order that new growth might be stimulated. However, this will only be achieved by exploring in ways which are manageable, sustainable and not shame-inducing.

Another key consideration for the supervisor here and indeed throughout the facilitation of all supervisory creative action methods is to maintain a clear supervisory focus. The supervisor works to guard against any inadvertent move into personal process. Clear facilitative holding of the method is key here to ensure that the inquiry remains supervisory, a reflection on practice rather than therapeutic and a personal process of the self. Once completed, the clockwise course moves the focus onwards to arrive in the south-western quadrant.

The Lower Left Quadrant – The Role of Creativity

In this quadrant the supervisor invites the supervisee to "make marks which reflect how creativity appears, guides and inspires you in your life". This is a broad and open invitation that connects with generalised notions of creative thinking, as well as acknowledging the influential role of more specific creative practice. I once explored this method with a supervisee who had not formed conscious connections between what they described as their "passionate hobby" of gardening and their clinical practice. The power of this appearing on the page through a series of spontaneous, innocent and unmistakable motifs was a moving and clarifying affirmation of that individual's personal style of practice.

The notion of 'creativity' can be problematic and daunting for some. We may often hear supervisees tell us that they are not creative. In making the initial invitation, be attentive to help your supervisee avoid their reflections being intruded upon by overthinking or the crushing self-critical expectations to produce a creative masterpiece! Keep the facilitation fluid and simple. Avoid complicating the instructions. Ask them to allow and trust their naturally arising thoughts and feelings to guide their hand in the mark-making. In this way, with uncomplicated facilitation, support them to work with an open and curious spirit. In following this approach, the supervisee may be able to translate something of their creative essence onto the paper through the act of spontaneous mark-making.

A Facilitative Option When Working 1:1

There is another facilitative option that can help explore '*the role of creativity*' when facilitating this method in a 1:1 context. This draws on the fourth shape instruction from the Six Shape Supervision Structure (6S) as described in Chapter 6.

As in the 6S method, here the supervisee is invited to 'take off' their thinking hat. The supervisor makes that same and particular intervention at this point to employ a gestural action, miming taking off a hat. The supervisee is directed to put their art materials to one side and mirror that which the supervisor now demonstrates – the two-handed lifting off and placing to one side of an imagined 'thinking hat'. This marks a playful, relieving and freeing moment in the process. Sometimes it may evoke laughter or a mildly self-conscious smile. It is a powerful relational moment. It also provides an exhalation from the focused intensity of the inquiry so far. It may bring some relief following the visiting of vulnerabilities in the previous quadrant. Free now of their 'thinking hat', the supervisee is directed to choose a mark-maker and to place the nib of it somewhere within this quadrant. Once placed the supervisee is invited to work unsighted. If comfortable they may close their eyes; otherwise they avert their gaze from the paper. The supervisor asks the supervisee to consider "the role of creativity in your practice". Help them avoid this reflection being intruded upon by overthinking or limited thoughts. Keep the facilitation fluid and simple. Avoid complicating the instructions. Ask them to allow the naturally arising thoughts and feelings to guide their hand in the mark-making. In this way, with uncomplicated facilitation, working unsighted and intuitively, the supervisee translates something of their creative essence onto the paper through the act of spontaneous mark-making.

The supervisor's facilitative sensitivity is especially called upon here to guide and observe but in ways which are appropriately modulated and measured. This can be quite nuanced. Apparently small and slight refinements can make a significant difference. During this quadrant, I often turn my head away from the working supervisee, so I see them only peripherally. This feels respectful and important both energetically and relationally as a way of honouring the spirit of non-intrusiveness and the safety of the creative space. I verbally conclude the process by inviting them to again open their eyes. Maintaining my peripheral posture and gaze, I leave them time and space to take in the marks that have appeared on the paper. Only then do I turn towards them again.

There is another concluding task to be completed before the leaving of this quadrant. The replacement of the 'thinking hat'. The supervisor reminds the supervisee of this and again guides them through miming/mirroring the action to replace the hat and to re-engage with their thinking function.

Coming Full Circle

The mark-making task is now complete, and the supervisee can sit back and take in, for the first time, the mandala in its entirety. Here is a unique, original and newly created piece of work that both captures and reflects back key aspects of the practitioner's practice and themselves. In order that the significance of this accomplishment can be sufficiently recognised, the supervisor may take a few moments before moving to the next step.

The supervisor next invites the supervisee to tell them about what has appeared on the paper before them to share what was behind the marks that have been made. The sequence for this descriptive and reflective sharing echoes the order that led to the creation of the piece. Quadrant by quadrant, the supervisee explains the meanings contained within their mark-making. The act of telling here may be significant. This within itself may provide new and hitherto unrealised insights as the work is brought to a fuller conscious awareness and new patterns, resonances and meanings become apparent. The supervisor may adopt the role of the listener to simply receive the supervisee's descriptions. They may at times also choose to reflect back something of value that occurs to them, but which might be otherwise overlooked by the supervisee.

I usually conclude the practice by inviting the supervisee to date their work. I offer the thought that it now exists as a 'snapshot' of them and their practice today, something that might be kept and looked back upon at a later time. This is especially useful for those supervisees who appear intrigued and chime with the potential value of mandala practice. I have worked with several supervisees who, having been introduced to this technique, have subsequently adopted the practice and created a *mandala journal* as a way of tracking and reflecting on their own practice journey. In this way, they mirror the way Jung took up the practice in 1916, following his own travails and the struggles he encountered in developing his work.

> I sketched every morning in a notebook a small circular drawing, a mandala, which seemed to correspond to my inner situation at the time. With the help of these drawings I could observe my psychic transformations from day to day.
>
> (Jung, 1989: 195)

Completing the Circle

In *The Mandala and Visions of Wholeness*, psychotherapist Rob Preece discusses the multifarious ways mandala practice reflects aspects of the mandala maker themselves. Preece writes,

> Each of us will orientate towards one of the functions as the dominant way in which we cognise the world … the two adjacent functions will be present but less active and one will remain predominantly in the unconscious. The map they create has many implications in our psychological life, our relationships and our work.
>
> (Preece, 2021: 29)

Similarly, the supervisory mandala will reflect those areas of an individual's practice which are strong and established. It will also reveal something of those which remain underdeveloped, in need of resourcing or which are being neglected. It might even provide indications towards aspects of practice which have hitherto remained entirely out of sight.

The two discrete approaches to working with a mandala in supervisory contexts can be used in a combined way, as outlined above or with each standing alone. In my own supervisory practice experience I most commonly facilitate the latter, paper-based technique for supervisees. Occasionally and mainly in the context of in-person settings, I will use both methods as an integrated whole. I have also used the embodied approach singularly as a method within and of itself. This has been prompted in work with supervisees who have a particular familiarity or an expressed wish to work in an embodied way and/or who practice within such modalities: somatic practitioners and dance movement psychotherapists.

Considerations When Using the Mandala Method Online

The two Mandala methods described above translate particularly well for online supervision sessions. Some advance preparation is required on behalf of your supervisee. Look to support them in a prior session to make any necessary arrangements ahead of the actual session. If you are looking to facilitate the embodied element, ensure there is sufficiently clear space available to allow your supervisee to move freely and safely. In planning to use the paper-based method, ask your supervisee to have a suitable piece of plain paper and to have drawing materials readily to hand.

If their technical equipment allows, ask them to adjust the direction of their camera to allow you as the supervisor to view the marks being made on the paper as they appear. This allows both yourself and your supervisee to feel more mutually present. It also means you can track the emergent process and make facilitatory interventions at timely junctures.

Be especially mindful to facilitate a clear and contained ending process when working online. Direct the ending sequentially step by step. I have found it useful to remain viewing together the various marks as they are being described by the supervisee in the shared reflective round, when the supervisee explains to the supervisor what informed their mark-making. So I usually prompt the move to readjust the camera back to face-to-face once that part of the technique has been completed. This signals the conclusion of the creative exercise. I invite them to pack away the drawing materials and place the mandala to one side. Once more face-to-face, I then initiate a more distanced and retrospective reflection. This could reach back to revisit the original supervisory question or ask for their thoughts about next steps or future considerations. This aims to complete their transition from the creative explorative space and back to a grounded and conscious presence as supervisee with their supervisor reflecting on current and onward practice.

Regarding the clear facilitation of this method be it in person or online, it is the continuing task of the supervisor to remain present and attentive throughout to work alongside the supervisee as a benign and supportive facilitating guide. Initiating, supporting and holding these emergent creative processes require care. They are often journeys into the as yet unknown. We do not know what will emerge and when or how. In your supervisory facilitation of the method aim to reflect such sensitivity; be alive to nuance and be comfortable with the unplanned, spontaneous and ambiguous communications that may surface. I have mentioned the considered use of a measured and diffused gaze. It is also helpful to observe not just what the supervisee does but *how* they work; the pauses, the immediacy, the pace and rhythm of their mark-making. Look to be aware and ready to consider any quadrants that may be especially full or any that are left mainly blank. Where space is left open, the proxemics of those marks, how they sit in relation to others, etc., may hold important information. The considerations and connecting of such observations may reveal critical formative aspects which can be explored more fully in onward supervision.

References

Bachelard, G., 1994. *The Poetics of Space*. Beacon Press.
Bousquet, J., 1989. *Le Menuer de Lune*. Éditions Albin Michel.
Jaspers, K., 1947. *Von der Wahrheit*. Piper.
Jennings, S., 1997. *Introduction to Dramatherapy, Theatre and Healing*. JKP.
Jones, P., 1996. *Drama as Therapy, Theatre as Living*. Routledge.
Jung, C., 1989. *Memories, Dreams and Reflections*. Vintage.
Preece, R., 2021. *The Mandala and Visions of Wholeness*. Mudra.
Rawson, P., 1995. *The Art of Tantra*. Thames and Hudson.
Sajnani, N., 2002. *The Embodied Mandala Method as an Assessment Tool in Drama Therapy*. https://spectrum.library.concordia.ca/id/eprint/1589/. Accessed 01 August 2024.
van Gogh, V., 1882. *Vincent van Gogh – The Letters*. https://vangoghletters.org/vg/letters/let249/letter.html. Accessed 31 July 2024.
White, L., 2002. *The Action Manual: Techniques for Enlivening Group Process and Individual Counselling*. Elizabeth White.

Chapter 11

The Framework for the Embodied Reflective Narrative

Céline Butté

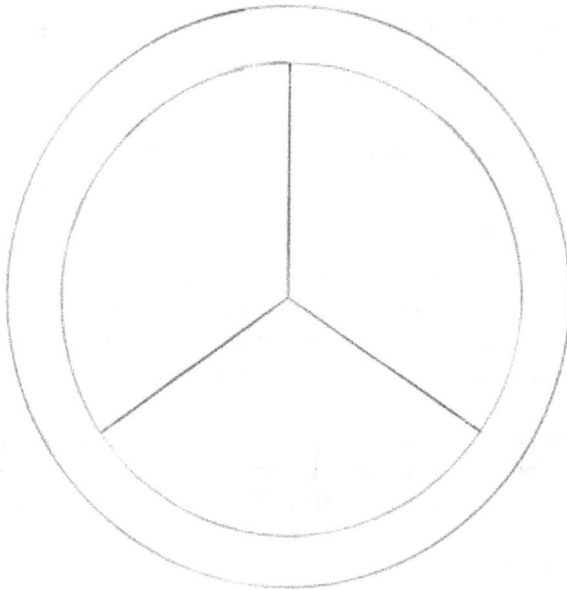

Figure 11.0

Imagine a fern in a forest, unfurling. Can you feel the release of such a moment? Can you sense your body letting go yet being fully present, open and receptive?

When developing the Framework for the Embodied Reflective Narrative (FERN), my intention was to bring together well-established and effective somatic awareness and movement tools to foster such a sensory and embodied quality of presence in service of the reflective and restorative aspects of supervision.

FERN is a reciprocal bottom-up, top-down approach to gaining insights and new knowledge. It favours the body, the domain of the senses and that of movement – however minimal and subtle – as the initial guide to our cognition and

DOI: 10.4324/9781003435655-14

meaning-making. If we consider human development, we know that moving and sensing precede talking. FERN invites us to get in touch with the wisdom embedded in these primordial ways of being. It is a technique that welcomes the less organised and thought-through parts of us. When using FERN, our cognitive capacity is engaged to notice what our body has noticed first.

In the context of conventional clinical practice, reflection is mostly understood as a verbal process that engages our mind; 'the mind' being recognised as "a person's ability to think and reason; the intellect" (Oxford Languages, 2025). We see in this definition that the mind is located within our head. By deduction reflection is predominantly understood as a cognitive process that happens in our head.

Although the above definition is the most widely acknowledged, the primary definition of 'the mind' is in fact more expansive and less localised. In its original definition, Oxford Languages (2025) characterises the mind as "the element of a person that enables them to be aware of the world and their experience, to think and to feel; the faculty of consciousness and thought". FERN leans on this original definition. I would in fact go further and use the word 'element' in its plural form 'elements' in this definition. This would more accurately acknowledge that our reflective capacity lives in our whole body – including our brain – but is not limited to cognition.

As an example of the various parts of our body that are party to our reflexive capacity, let us consider our enteric nervous system, an independent nervous system located in our gastrointestinal tract that deals with digestion. Whilst it is indeed true that this system supports the breaking down of the food that we eat, it is also home to a great number of alchemical processes that enable us to digest our experience. Our enteric nervous system is therefore connected to our emotions, mood and decision-making and so is implicated in the subjectivity of our experience and consequently in our reflexivity. It is in fact often referred to as our second brain or 'gut brain'. I would argue that the enteric nervous system might actually be an original location of knowing that FERN invites us to make space for.

Simply to exist is an embodied felt experience. Therefore, theoretically, FERN is informed by mindfulness as an embodied practice, in particular as experienced in Authentic Movement (Adler, 2002) and by Embodied Performances, a feminist research and practice methodology developed by Allegranti (2011). More on the origins of FERN can be found in an earlier publication (Butté, 2023).

FERN sets out to address the invisible marks our work leaves on or even within us. We impact and are impacted by our environment and relationships, although we may remain unaware of the imprint we leave on each other. In our busy lives, we do not necessarily take the time or have opportunities to acknowledge how a person (a client or colleague), a place (a work environment) or a system (our client's family or the policies that guide our practice in a specific setting) affects us. We say that we are touched by a client's story, that some aspects of our work get hooked in us, and that we find ourselves unable to speak in a colleague's presence. Can you hear these metaphorical definitions of the (professional) relationships? All these images exist in movement, and they can be re-presented, embodied as a shape or posture, for example. FERN affords us a creative opportunity to suspend time and step into a moment of slowing our cognition down, to bring our physical experience to the fore and let our moving and sensing body lead the way. This is the embodied narrative that FERN invites. It is a narrative because essentially, a moving body tells a story.

FERN was developed and refined over many years of supervision practice. It is best understood as a supervision tool or technique within which sits a circular physical framework, a mandala (see Chapter 10 for more on mandalas) which I will refer to as the FERN map hereafter. The FERN map is made of four distinct and connected zones. Entitled 'Self', 'Relationship', 'Bigger Picture' and 'Observer/ Witness', these zones become the containers of an improvised piece of dance movement. By letting their spontaneous physical resonance with their work unfurl, the supervisee finds their way straight to the heart of what needs attending to. As Barnstaple reminds us, "embodying something, whether consciously chosen or spontaneous and reflected upon afterwards, has the immediate power to take us to an intimacy with our experience and emotions" (Barnstaple cited in Williams, 2022: 103).

FERN may be used once the supervisee is clear about their supervisory question or theme. At this point, the supervisor and supervisee transition from their seated position and the supervisor guides their supervisee to lay out a circular map containing the four zones. These are delineated on the ground by props such as scarves or long strips of ribbon. Three of the zones are entitled Self, Relationship and Bigger Picture. These are located within a central disc in three segments of equal size, large enough for the supervisee to sit or stand in. This central disc is surrounded by an outer ring, known as the Observer/Witness zone.

In the Observer/Witness zone, supervisees are invited to let the ripples from the more activating investigative zones of Self, Relationship and Bigger Picture percolate. This outer zone is a reminder to stay with the inner inquiry and immediacy of activation that the inner circle potentially invites. It also provides safety in the process by offering a way in and out of the central three zones and can be returned to for self-regulation whenever needed.

This map, with its four clearly delineated zones, functions as a stage onto which the supervisee steps and through which they move spontaneously in relation to a particular supervisory enquiry. Stepping into this structure is often surprisingly powerful and any non-stylised spontaneous movement that emerges draws our interest and attention (sounds and words are welcome, too). The movement that arises can offer insights that enable us to make sense of what is going on in relation to the supervisory question or theme.

The time spent within the FERN map is immersive for the supervisee. The supervisor never enters nor adjusts the framework for the supervisee but remains outside of the map throughout, attuning to the supervisee's process. In this way, the supervisor creates an environment conducive to the spontaneous expression of the supervisee.

Bringing FERN to Life

Here we are, standing in front of the FERN map now set up on the ground. During your exploration within this map, you are free to move where your feet take you and to spend as much and as little time in each of the four zones. Just let the body respond with open curiosity and consider what gestures might be relevant. You might want to experiment with accentuating or diminishing your movement at times.

First of all, however, please take a moment to walk through the framework to clarify which segment you are choosing for the zones of Self, Relationship and Bigger Picture. You can name these, so we are both clear. Or you can place an object in each segment to remind us both of your choice.

Next, let's take a moment to stand outside of the map and remind ourselves of your supervisory question. As we stand here, you can now let go of holding your question in your mind and trust that it is held in your body. Let's now take a moment of preparation.

Within the zone of Self take a moment to be 'with' and give shape to the different selves relevant to your supervisory question. This may include yourself as therapist or coach, but importantly it may also include the self of your client or of other individuals relevant to the piece of work you are exploring today.

In the zone of Relationship, allow yourself to sense in your body and through your posture any possible relational dynamic relevant to your supervisory question. For example, if you would like to explore the tense relationship between your client and their mother, you may take a moment in this zone to give shape to this tension and feel into what this evokes in you.

The Bigger Picture segment is where you may consider the socio-political context and environmental factors relevant to your question. This may be a particular system such as your client's family, their culture or the organisation you work for. National, international and global events may also be relevant in this zone.

You can travel out of the inner three segments into the Observer/Witness zone to take a pause from what you connect with in the Self, Relationship and Bigger Picture segments –, catch your breath and regulate. When in the Observer/Witness zone, pay attention to what is going on in yourself as well as within the rest of the structure, with gentle curiosity. When you step in this zone, you may choose to walk or sit down for a moment, maybe close your eyes to listen in more fully with kindness and without judgement.

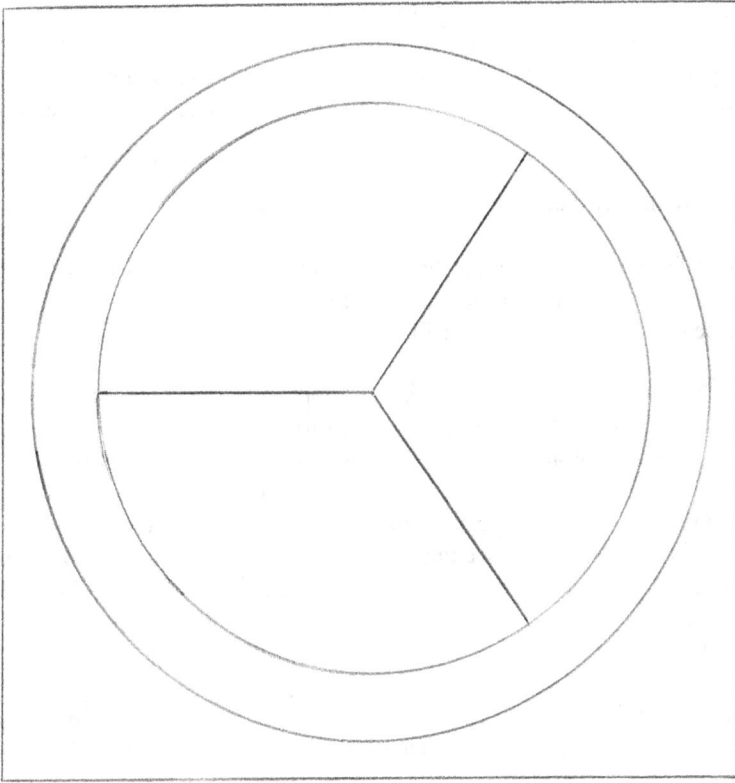

Figure 11.1 Basic map for FERN

In my experience, there comes a moment when the supervisee looks towards me and indicates that this part of their exploration within the FERN map feels complete. At this point, I invite them to step outside of the map. We take a moment to stand next to each other, both looking towards the FERN map laid out on the ground. Following this pause, the supervisee has a first opportunity to reflect on what has unfolded during their time within the FERN map and to speak to what came up for them. Having listened to the supervisee, I can now offer my initial reflections; it is helpful to be literal and inquisitive rather than interpretative at this point. For example, "I noticed that you didn't go into the zone of 'Bigger Picture' and wonder what this is about", or "it was interesting to see that you looked down when in the zone of Self and that you were looking around when in the zone of Relationship. Does this mean anything to you?" It can be enlightening for supervisees to have these broader patterns of postures and movement across the FERN map reflected back to them. This helps them to make sense of what is more unconsciously held within them at a physical, non-verbal level and offers further opportunities to engage their cognitive and verbal reflective capacity. Being reminded of a particular sequence of movement in a specific segment of the FERN map might be all they need to make sense of something that had so far eluded them.

There are now two options:

Option 1: The supervisee deroles the FERN map. Supervisor and supervisee return to their original seated position, ready for final reflections on 'what next' and maybe on how it has felt to use FERN.

Option 2: The supervisee is given a final opportunity to revisit a specific part or parts of the FERN map as a way of refining a line of inquiry or to consolidate a particular insight. Although this second round within the FERN map may be quite brief, it can serve as a useful way to locate an insight within a particular segment of the map to anchor it in the body for future recollection. Once this is complete, the supervisee is invited to derole the FERN map and supervisor and supervisee can transition back to their original seated position to proceed with final reflections as just described in Option 1 above.

Using a technique such as FERN for the first time can be compared to deep-sea diving. One does not just go deep-sea diving (stepping into the FERN map): there is a process of getting accustomed to the water (the FERN map), to the breathing equipment (the props) and to the language of diving and the sense of the body's natural buoyancy in water (letting the body sense its way through the map and allowing spontaneous movement). Every step though is immersive and has its own value. It is ok and even important to experiment with FERN as much as one is comfortable with. Some creative embodied practitioners might indeed go deep-sea diving right away because they recognise something familiar with FERN. Others will first need to dip their toe in, experiment with the equipment and feel their way through the map, its potential and potency.

Reflections from a Supervisee of Supervision

FERN is a creative, embodied method that I like to adopt. Its form and structure allow me to gently tap into what is contained in my body. The different spaces laid out on the floor enable thoughts and feelings to reach a level of consciousness where I can filter out therapeutic processing – thus enabling clarity and expansion in my work and helping to form and crystallise my ideas as a supervisor and supervisee.

This method also takes my supervisee Helena closer towards understanding what's going on in the therapeutic space with her client, a 7-year-old boy diagnosed with autism. Helena is concerned about his emotional regulation. "He operates like an intricate and quick data-gathering computer system". Her supervisory question is, "How do I open his barriers and turn off his security system?" By exploring each zone, breathing and sensing into what resonated via the body, I witness Helena and offer guidance. Yet I also need to be discreet, almost invisible. Helena steps into each zone, allowing space and silence to connect with what is present. When her eyes are closed, Helena goes deeper into a sensorial mode of interoception. In the zone of Self, Helena shares, "my throat gets stuck when asking emotional questions". She recognises her sensitivity to her client's inability to relate emotionally. This somatic resonance is felt in her own voice. In the Relationship zone she says, "my heart feels vibrant and happy in this space". She notes how this reassures her as she recognises that the therapeutic relationship is indeed established. In the Bigger Picture, she shares, "I feel that I collude too much with his family, I feel guilty about this". This realisation enables her to recognise that she can make some adjustments to engage with the previously unconscious material that has just come to light. In the Observer/Witness zone, Helena says, "I believe I need not to push too much. We will be able to arrive at an emotional answer at the right time."

The inquiry takes place over 30 minutes. Helena clears all the materials away before we gather for final reflection. Helena concludes, "Pushing will only block the process, so I will respect that changes occur at the right moment."

Paula Grech, Dance Movement Psychotherapist and Supervisor, France and UK.

FERN invites somatic awareness that can be accessed from a still, seated position as well as reflection through movement. Somatic awareness and movement are two distinct and complementary ways of tapping into the body's wisdom. Some supervisees will naturally favour the somatic realm as a way of making sense of what they are holding in their body in relation to their practice. In this instance, once the framework is created on the ground and each zone is allocated its function: inner circle with 'Self', 'Relationship' and 'Bigger Picture' and outer circle for Observer/

Witness, the supervisee can place a chair in each zone. The supervisee is then invited to sit in a chair of their choice for a moment and sense what is there within themselves when sitting in a particular chair. They may then move to another chair within the frame and, once settled in that chair, notice what is evoked in them somatically in this new zone. They proceed from one chair to another following their intuition, until they feel their exploration is complete. This way of using the FERN map can be enlightening and will be enough for some. Simply walking through the frame and taking a moment in each of the segments, in no particular order, also offer insights. On occasions, the supervisor may invite the supervisee to consider the questions, "What moves you?" or "What are you sitting with in relation to your question?".

From the perspective of the well-established Seven-Eye supervision model (Hawkins and Shohet, 2009), or more specifically the Eight-Eye revised model as presented in this book (Chapter 3), FERN is a useful technique to work with all the Eyes. It lends itself particularly well for Eye Three and Eye Four as an embodied process that enables the supervisee to be with relational dynamics, ambiguity, transference and countertransference. Through movement they can 'not know' for a while, whether what they are feeling or embodying is their own or their client's 'stuff'. Thus, they can play with what is with(in) them, and feelings and sensations can be expressed and met. As the supervisee spends time within each zone of the FERN map, they get in touch with how their work 'hooks' and stays in their body. As they find the space to let these physical experiences speak, they may gradually disentangle the threads of something that they did not even know they had been holding. With the benefit of this information, the supervisee may be able to discern more clearly what might be theirs from what might be their client's. In this way, the FERN map helps identify fresh ways to return to their practice. FERN is also a good technique to work with Eye Seven, as the bigger picture surrounding an enquiry can be located in a specific segment and explored through postures, gestures and somatic tracking within that specific zone. FERN is a useful technique even in the smallest of spaces.

Whilst I have been describing the use of FERN with an individual, it may also be used with groups. In the context of group supervision, the supervisor may choose to work with an individual supervisee whilst the rest of the group sits outside of the FERN map and witnesses the piece of work. Alternatively, the supervisor may invite the whole group to use the FERN map simultaneously, once all have clarified their supervision question. If working with the whole group simultaneously, it is essential to have a fairly big space to allow movement within each of the zones.

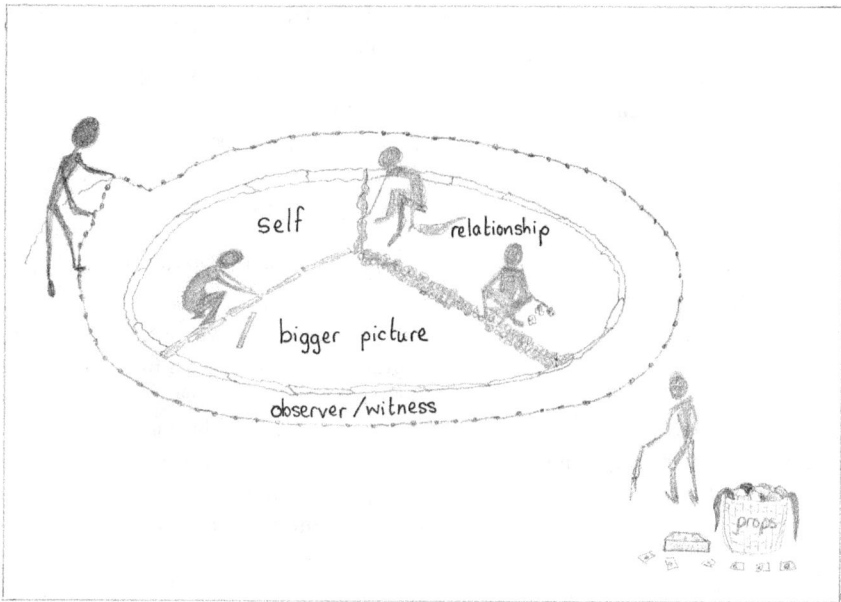

Figure 11.2 FERN in group work

Using FERN Online and Outdoors

Besides its application in the more conventional in-person settings of clinics and studios, FERN may be used online or outdoors. Micro-movement and somatic awareness, as described above with the use of chairs, are rich physical resources that sit well within this methodology and framework. To use FERN online, supervisees will need to have enough floorspace to stand, move and change posture as well as their own resources (in the form of props such as long strips of ribbons or several scarves) to create the FERN map.

For supervision practice outdoors, supervisor and supervisee take a moment to identify a possible location (please refer to Chapter 13 for more on outdoor practice). Natural structures such as a circle of trees or a brook may lend themselves well to represent some of the map's thresholds. The supervisee may also gently mark the ground with fallen leaves, twigs, stones or the soil itself to delineate both circles and the inner three segments. At the point of deroling the map (as described above), the supervisee clears the mandala away, leaving the place as they had found it on arrival.

Each human encounter is filled with a somewhat messy entanglement of feelings held, projected and at times disowned in a unique elusive constellation. As supervisees step into the FERN map, they locate and maybe organise what they are holding unconsciously, physically and somatically in relation to a specific supervisory question or theme. In the specific locations or zones the supervisee moves to and from, three levels are considered: the level of identity in the zone of Self, the relational level in the zone of Relationship, and the overall Bigger Picture specific to the piece of work. The supervisee proceeds within the map, allowing their body to 'show up' in a particular segment, letting themselves feel and sense 'what is present' at this particular level of experience. In the fourth 'Observer/Witness' zone, the supervisee recognises the magnitude or in fact the necessary subtlety of what might have been felt or 'touched' in one of the other three segments. The distancing this fourth zone offers attends to the safety of working with deep embodied processes.

Through FERN, one step at a time, supervisees disentangle the confusing threads contained in their inquiry and land with what is. Here, the fern fronds unfurl so that the condition, colour and texture of the process of their work are gradually revealed. Equipped with insights now anchored within themselves, the supervisee's practice transforms, and they often feel revitalised.

This chapter complements an earlier piece of writing on FERN (Butté, 2023) that offers more information on the origins of this method and some tools on working with movement and the body in supervision. Recent conversations with the LCP Creative Supervision Diploma teaching team and trainees have nourished further attention to the languaging and facilitation of this technique, which I hope makes its reach as broad as it was originally intended. I am grateful for their inquiry and reflections as they help me further refine and articulate this creative supervision method.

References

Adler, J., 2002. *Offering from the Conscious Body: The Discipline of Authentic Movement.* Inner Traditions.

Allegranti, B., 2011. *Embodied Performances: sexuality, gender, bodies.* Palgrave Macmillan.

Butté, C., 2023. "Reflections on Thresholds and Containers in Supervision". In Butté, C., and Colbert, N., eds., *Embodied Approaches to Supervision: The listening body.* Routledge.

Hawkins, P., and Shohet, R., 2009. *Supervision in the Helping Professions.* Open University Press.

Oxford Languages, 2025. "Mind". [Available at www.google.com/search?client=saf ari&rls=en&q=define+mind&ie=UTF-8&oe=UTF-8] (Accessed 9 March 2025).

Williams, C., 2022. *Move. The New Science of Body over Mind.* Profile Books Ltd.

Part III

Supervision Beyond the Clinic

Chapter 12

Supervision Beyond the Clinic

Anna Chesner, Céline Butté and Bryn Jones

Figure 12.0

DOI: 10.4324/9781003435655-16

Reflective Practice in the Arts, Education and Organisations

Why supervise beyond the clinic? Most of the examples in Part II have related to clinical or coaching practice. Although process supervision has emerged from the field of psychotherapy, the need to have a space to take stock and to reflect is in no way unique to clinical settings and is in fact true to good practice in all areas of work. Let us consider what is happening around us currently, by looking at various sectors.

Supervision for Teachers and School Teams

In schools' leadership teams, teachers and teaching assistants are having to manage and be responsible not only for teaching and classroom management, but also for elements of early development that are being less attended to at home for whatever reason. They are facing the reality of children's basic needs no longer being met. This means they cannot assume that children arrive at school clean, rested and fed having come from an adequate and stable housing situation. These children may not be able to toilet themselves and may carry the emotional burden of struggling families and communities. Behaviourally they may not be able to play socially, and their attention span may be severely diminished by an addictive relationship to their phones and social media, through which they are bombarded by information and misinformation they are not actively seeking. These multifarious and overwhelming challenges now commonly faced by school-aged young people are well documented by Jonathan Haidt in his book *The Anxious Generation* (Haidt, 2024). Haidt describes a profound and in his view disastrous recent shift from a play-based to a phone-based childhood. This he argues is leading to an epidemic of mental illness amongst young people, much of which will be apparent and require support within the school and learning environments they attend. Added to this are the ongoing increases in gang-related knife crime (ONS & BKT, 2024) and child-on-child abuse (The Observer, 2024). The effects of these frequently appear in school settings, often requiring urgent address and containment. These troubling trends are further underpinned by the modelling and legitimising of coercive and controlling relationships by influencers and others who hold power. The pervasive intensity of these developments is disrupting the traditional roles within child–parent, parent–school and child–school relationships. At the same time research and advocacy have facilitated the diagnosis of more young people as neurodivergent, and the expectation is that individualised adjustments are made within learning environments. Unmet and often undiagnosed mental health challenges of many young people or their parents complicate matters further. Even within the primary task of education, artificial intelligence (AI) is rapidly challenging existing norms and will continue to do so in ways we are presently unable to imagine. Teachers are facing an infinitely expanding demand to be up to date and aware of emerging trends and to respond and intervene in a timely and appropriate way to a changing world.

While supervision will not fix any of the underlying causes of these issues it can support those at the front line who face the effects of such multidimensional challenges on a daily basis. If the demands are unsustainable staff choose to leave or to remain but are then susceptible to burnout. In this context supervision offers a means to support staff well-being and retention. Action-based and creative supervision in particular mitigates against a hopeless and helpless mindset by activating creativity and playfulness in the reflective space.

Supervision for Head Teachers

Helen Yates, a graduate of the LCP Creative Supervision Training, reflects here on her supervision work with education staff.

> I initially took the Creative Approaches to Supervision training specifically to work with educational staff in a school setting. Supervision within education has become increasingly common, as there is an acknowledgement that senior leaders need a confidential reflective space to attend to the growing complexities of educational settings. Currently the charity Education Support offers short-term supervision for senior leaders in education, and the social enterprise Talking Heads offers long term supervision, also for senior leaders in education. I am proud to be working with both these organisations and believe that the support we offer benefits the entire system, especially the young people.

Helen goes on to reflect on which supervisory roles are emphasised in her work.

> I find myself very much in the role of supervisor as facilitator in these sessions, in order to give space to what needs to be reflected on and worked through. Initially, however, I inhabit the role of supervisor as teacher in order to educate the supervisee about the potential of the supervision space. This is particularly true when introducing creative methods. I learned early on in the process that the use of creative techniques encourages a potential vulnerability that needs to be respected and prepared for.

We are aware that the convention for these sessions is that they happen online and often from the supervisees' work setting. Helen faces the double challenge of introducing them to supervision as a frame for productive reflection and also to creative methods as an appropriate medium for this reflection. Senior leaders are required to be creative in their work but may not often find themselves within a frame that supports and activates their creativity.

> I support my supervisees to activate their imagination in relation to their professional challenges and goals. As they become more accustomed to the creative approaches, I have found Small World (Chapter 4) to be particularly useful in working through institutional and staff dynamics. On one occasion I worked

with a supervisee who had lost access to their self-confidence. I offered the Mandala method (Chapter 10) which helped them reconnect with their skills and creative abilities as a leader.

This is a good example of the restorative function of the Mandala technique and of the importance of supervision within a demanding, overwhelming organisation and educational system. As Helen says above, helping the leaders also brings a positive impact to the lives of the staff team and the young people. While Mandala as a technique focuses on what we have termed Eye Eight (Chapter 3), the relationship of the self to the work and the alignment of the work with the individual's core values, its benefits may radiate out into the system as a whole.

More information on the availability of supervision in education can be found on the following websites. www.educationsupport.org.uk and https://talkingheads supervision.co.uk.

Supervision for CICs and the Voluntary Sector

Over recent years the services provided by local government have been affected by cuts to their budgets and consequent service closures or reductions. This puts an added burden on the voluntary sector (i.e. charities, Community Interest Companies (CICs) and other community initiatives). People working in this sector come face-to-face with people in need and human distress. Not having been trained as therapists, they will not necessarily have had therapy themselves and yet will come into contact with people and communities in crisis and displaying acute need. They may not have the resilience-enhancing training that therapists have, including ongoing therapy and supervision. Such practitioners may receive occasional training such as safeguarding, trauma-informed practice, health and safety or first aid, but that kind of training provision does not attend to the ongoing process of being faced with human distress and trauma. In order for people to do this work in a way that is sustainable, healthy and kind to self, regular supervision, as distinct from line management, is, arguably, essential. As a supervisee from one of these settings said, "supervision offers a relief from the perpetual give give give energy and a time for pausing, releasing, putting down and making sense" (anonymous supervisee, personal communication).

Stephen Mulley, a graduate of the LCP Creative Supervision Training, reflects on his work as a supervisor with non-clinical administrative staff within a therapeutic fostering and adoption service. He writes

I have found the supervision of non-clinical administrative staff to be challenging and fascinating. In our setting, the admin team roles involve far more than just admin! For example, they have regular phone, email and face to face communication with parents who are stressed, exhausted, distressed, upset and worried.

They are often in the office when therapists come out of clinical sessions. They attend team-wide clinical supervision sessions. In all of these ways they are exposed to the emotional and psychological responses and dynamics that play out across the service in response to the very impactful clinical material. In addition to this they liaise with other services whose staff are also often stressed, exhausted, distressed, upset and worried. Therefore, my supervision must address their social encounters and the emotional and psychological impact of these. They may come to me with examples of situations they have experienced, interactions they have had, or moments they have witnessed that they do not understand or have the skills to process. I need to allow for, encourage, and hold emotional reactions to this material which we attempt to process and work through. This is not something they are necessarily used to, experienced in, or trained for. It can feel unfamiliar and uncomfortable.

This account of the setting gives a vivid example of the need for a reflective space for non-clinical staff and how much these staff members are holding. As with Helen above, Stephen needs to adopt the role of supervisor as teacher as well as facilitator.

My role also involves education around psychological processes, as the admin team is not trained in this. I notice that I have to do this far more than with clinically trained supervisees. Currently my main non-clinical supervisee leads one of the admin teams, so she provides supervision to them. This also means that part of my role is supporting her in her holding of the processes the admin team brings to her. There is an element of upskilling and disseminating knowledge.

Supervision within the Humanitarian Charity Sector

Anna has been giving regular supervision over a number of years to a humanitarian charity, delivering frontline services to people with vulnerabilities, at risk of being excluded from healthcare settings. The model includes regular one-to-one supervision for team members as well as for the service delivery manager. From time to time this is complemented by team supervision sessions. In this discussion with 'A', the service delivery manager, we begin by reflecting on the nature of the service and the benefits of supervision within such a service. 'A' articulates the need for supervision:

Any front line worker, and any organisation working in this field is exposed to significant levels of trauma on a daily basis. The reflective space provided by supervision reduces the risk of vicarious trauma. The need is all the more acute when employing someone with lived experience. As a small to medium sized charity, we are always exposed to funding and financial pressures, which are exacerbated at times of political and social change. Staff are often stretched to the limit of their capacity. Even though charities do their best to maintain wellbeing in the staff group there is nonetheless the risk of moral injury. For example, if a front-line worker has had their particular service cut there are painful questions about why one part of the service is valued above others. It is the front-line workers who are most acutely aware of the impact of such changes on the service users.

We acknowledge that those drawn to humanitarian work with vulnerable groups, whether they fall under the category of having lived experience or not, often have some form of traumatic experience in their background which inspires them to make a difference. Working in this kind of setting can be a way of sublimating and attempting to recover from such experiences. Judith Herman in her book on trauma sees this community-oriented action, which she names "Reconnection" as part of the third phase of trauma work (Herman, 1992).

While the team is close knit, and the dedication of its members has led to a stability in staffing over several years, we reflect on 'A''s promotion to the role of service delivery manager and how supervision has supported this change of role.

'A' says:

Supervision has provided a space to look at my relationship to both senior management and service delivery. The higher up the organisation you rise the more responsible you feel and are for the wellbeing of the team, the delivery of the services and the health of the organisation. Supervision has been a space to reflect on strategy, and to work through any emotional challenges that arise in relation to interpersonal staff dynamics. This was particularly useful when it came to my need to develop new roles and responsibilities with former peers.

From Anna's perspective, it has been important to hold the confidentiality of the individual supervisees, whilst also bearing in mind the differing roles and needs within the team. On those occasions when there have been group supervision sessions these have been useful in terms of allowing the multiple points of view to be heard and witnessed by all present. These sessions have allowed differences to be acknowledged in an accepting environment, which in turn has led to more group cohesion.

Thinking about the impact of the creative methods in the supervision of this organisation 'A' reports that they have been helpful for her personally in mapping out complex systems and strategies, by the use of concretisation and Small World. They have particularly helped in group supervision sessions, where the playfulness and apparent levity of the method have facilitated working through some difficult situations. "It has given a safe language to look at complex problems. Symbolism helps shift things; an object expresses more than you might be able to put into words".

Anna adds to this that the creation of something visual and tangible in the team supervision sessions gives more presence to what has been articulated by team members. While words that are spoken remain present in an invisible way, the concrete co-created sculpt keeps the different contributions visibly in mind, in a third space, separate from and shared by the team member until this is collectively deroled towards the end of a session.

Supervision in the Creative Industries

In the creative industries there is an interface between the art itself and wider society. There are theatre companies, for example, who specialise in running performances and workshops within the education or forensic settings. External requirements for accessing grants add an extra pressure to the planning, delivery and evidencing of such projects. During the delivery itself staff come into contact with people, material and dynamics that can be challenging and are often destabilising. Supervision can provide an environment to reflect, reset and restore balance to individuals and groups working in these settings.

Creativity thrives on pushing boundaries and being edgy. At the same time there are welcome changes in the creative industries that challenge the normalisation of exploitative power games and abuse. This is evidenced by the ubiquity of intimacy co-ordinators and well-being or counselling services that companies are now expected to provide.

Even in the training of performers and creative practitioners there is added pressure to take appropriate care of trainees. The playfulness of the rehearsal room benefits from being free, but the limits of that freedom can be a point of contention, conflict and pain. Lecturers and trainers may carry an additional anxiety about what is okay and where the limits are in the current changing climate.

Supervision offers a space to explore the multiple perspectives of difficult moments in training and rehearsal and to mitigate against the risk of polarisation and escalation and the consequent potential recourse to complaints or legal procedures. It allows the practitioner to find an appropriate sense of proportion in their actions and responses and the space to explore and attend to the perceptions and sensibilities of others they are working with.

Performance, perhaps particularly theatre performance, has an intrinsic therapeutic potential. Performers who have a particular life experience, often traumatic, may choose this medium to give form to and share their personal autobiographical experiences. It can be profoundly validating to be witnessed in such a piece of work. Both the creative process and the performance can reduce the debilitating sense of shame and aloneness that often accompanies trauma. The creative process of such pieces of work involves a degree of courage and can create challenging emotional moments for the whole creative team. Here again, supervision can offer a unique space to process, reflect and reset.

Supervision for an Arts Organisation

Let us hear the different perspectives from two creative practitioners, Suha Al-Khayyat and Alex Cooke, co-artistic directors and senior managers of Little

Fish Theatre Company. Each of them is supervised by a different member of the writing team for this book and their reflections highlight both their differences in how they use supervision as well as the impact on the company as a whole of creative supervision being available at the senior leadership team level. By having a separate space to reflect, Suha and Alex are able to work together in partnership in ways that are healthy and dialogic as a mini-team at the top of the organisation.

Suha reflects "Supervision is a helpful resource to support what can sometimes feel like an overwhelming work schedule. It allows space to prioritise what is important, to discuss this and work through the material systematically".

Suha's supervisor, Anna, notes that the kind of material that arises in supervision with Suha varies. Sometimes the priority is the wider dimension of fund-raising applications and their impact on future programme planning. On other occasions the focus is on the narrower specifics of staffing dynamics for a particular project or the creative process of writing or directing new pieces.

Suha continues:

> Challenges with workload, staffing and the creative process can be talked through, and strategies to deal with issues are explored in as much depth as is needed. It is a supportive environment where successes are acknowledged, good models of practice are celebrated, and the smooth running of projects are analysed to capture what is working and why. My supervisor also highlights working patterns that are not working so well and poses questions which challenge my set ways of thinking.

Anna reflects that the balance of support and challenge is as important in the creative artistic supervisory setting as it is in clinical work. Suha goes on to reflect on the specifics of working creatively in the supervision space. Techniques that have become part of our shared supervisory vocabulary include Small World and larger-scale concretisation.

Creative supervision has supported my personal work with Little Fish and the organisation as a whole. On a personal level, my role involves juggling multiple creative and administrative projects. I find it particularly engaging to use 'play' whilst discussing staff dynamics. To physically see the people, I am talking about represented by objects, sometimes figurines or toys, allows both myself and my supervisor to see where the relationships are placed. I position these props symbolically, bearing in mind closeness and distance as well as scale. Recently, I used creative supervision to map out the scenes of a new play I am writing. This made it easier to talk about it, particularly as there are over twenty different characters. By concretising the plot and character relationships, I could see where the strengths and weaknesses of the play were and discuss with my supervisor what needs to be worked on and prioritised.

The concretised image of the plot allowed us to look at structural choices in the play, when and if certain characters need to be used at all. I recall another writing project where the concretisation helped with visualising design options for staging.

Suha continues, " ... we can use the props to facilitate talking about the project on a broader scale, politically and socially. On a personal level, it is interesting to see which creative objects I seem to gravitate towards and what they mean to me".

Finally, Suha reflects on a special session in which I worked with both co-directors in their office with a focus on bigger picture planning for the company:

We worked on how Little Fish runs on a wider scale. It was useful to look at the roles and responsibilities we both have, and to do this with the help of an impartial third party. This forged a space to look at the successes of the company and where the gaps are. It was helpful to map out Little Fish activities together. Through this work we were able to create a new job role of producer to support all company members and to determine what we wanted to do more and less of.

Alex, writer and artistic co-director of Little Fish Theatre Company, adds

As a writer and director of a theatre company that creates work with and for young people, I am currently developing a new production that explores youth justice and gender-based violence. I am due to meet with my board of governors to reflect on the impact and intentionality behind the project. Our aim is to present these issues in theatrically powerful ways that provoke immediate, authentic responses from young audiences – responses that can then be unpacked in follow-up workshops and discussions. Throughout my professional career, I have accessed many forms of external supervision – from management consultants to life coaches to clinical supervisors. Each has offered something distinct, but creative approaches to supervision enable a greater explorative depth of enquiry.

Bryn, Alex's supervisor reflects, I am often struck by this in the supervisory process with Alex. He will bring a clear and discernible starting point for the supervisory enquiry which quickly appears to grow expansive. The subsequent enquiry involves reviewing options, testing potential outcomes and imagining their consequences and further implications.

Alex says

Creative approaches allow for a more rigorous interrogation – not only of our methods but of the assumptions and privileges that I and the company may bring to the work. That kind of reflective scrutiny hasn't emerged as easily in other types of supervision I've experienced. Creative and reflective supervision has also offered a valuable space to examine the ethics of our approach. While the intention is to engage and educate, the emotional impact of witnessing such material – particularly for young audiences – must be carefully considered. Supervision has helped me hold the tension between responsibility and artistic integrity: how do we create work that is sensitive and ethical, but that doesn't dilute or deflect the severity of the issues we're exploring?

Bryn concludes, it seems there is something here in being able to step back from the aliveness and urgency of these events themselves and to reconsider them through aesthetically distanced lenses and more reflective perspectives. To my mind, it is often by siting them in the distinct and delineated space of creative supervision that a critical, purposeful and clarified examination might be possible.

Supervision within the Church, Chaplaincy, Education Context

Jane Leach, another graduate of the LCP Creative Supervision Training, works in the field of Christian theological education and since 2004 has been offering supervision and training supervisors specifically to work with clergy, chaplains and theological educators across a variety of Christian denominations and in multi-faith contexts.

Jane shares

> From 2007-2009 I was part of a group of church leaders, theological educators, healthcare chaplains and counsellors with an interest in supporting clergy, that formed the Association of Pastoral Supervision and Education (https://media. methodist.org.uk/media/documents/conf-2021-40-reflective-supervision-rep ort_QurVZWc.pdf) to accredit and regulate a growing community of pastoral supervisors. The founding of a professional association grew from the recognition of the need for supervision that supports the wellbeing of ministry practitioners in the UK, safeguards the welfare of those the churches engage with, and offers regular space for learning and growth.

In the UK the first religious body to require its ministers to be in regular supervision was the Methodist Church. This was prompted by the findings of its voluntary past cases review into instances of bullying and abuse in an attempt not only to deal with outstanding or unreported cases but also to learn the lessons of the past.
  It concluded

> What is evident from many of the cases reported to the PCR is that the culture of the church was made unsafe, not only by the actions of the perpetrators, but also by the subsequent actions of those in authority or in colleague relationships who have failed to respond in a way that recognises the reality of the abuse that has taken place.
>
> (Methodist Conference Past Cases Review, 2015: 20)

Twenty-three recommendations were made to help the church become a safer place for everyone and help move the church from a place of isolated and sometimes vulnerable practice towards a culture of supported accountability for safe practice. The most far-reaching recommendation was number 7:

> That a system of structured supervision for ministers be instituted to address the identified weakness in relation to accountability and support in terms of safe practice.
>
> (2015: 27)

> It was not argued in the 2015 Report that supervision would be a panacea that would on its own eliminate abuse from church life, but that it would contribute to a change of culture.
>
> (Methodist Conference Supervision Report, 2017: § 2.1)

In 2016 Jane was appointed to oversee the implementation of a system of structured supervision, initially for some two thousand clergy and then for an equal number of lay ministers in designated roles. The learning from this process is explored in Leach 2020.

Following a major piece of research published in its 2021 Reflective Supervision Report, the Methodist Church concluded:

> In summary, the overwhelming evidence is that where the policy is being implemented the benefits are in line with those identified as aims in the 2017 report, and that it is beginning to establish a culture of ministry that is less isolated and vulnerable and safer for everyone involved.
>
> (Methodist Conference Reflective Supervision Report, 2021: § 4.4.4)

One of the things that is impressive about this particular implementation of supervision beyond the clinic is that it has expanded internationally and to a variety of different churches and related institutions.

Jane reflects that in all these settings the stress and isolation of clergy has been a significant motivation for introducing supervision, and the experience of supervision has been seen to have a significant impact on that stress. For example, the Revd Silas Muriithi commented in a feedback session on the training he received in Kenya after two years' experience:

> I came to realise that so many ministers are suffering issues with depression and burnouts because many times we think we are the ones having the solutions to people's problems. I have come to realise that I am not the one who should give people solutions to their problems. I have realised that everyone person has a solution to the problems they are suffering, but only when they are given that empowerment and given an opportunity to look into themselves. Now I am able to help them resolve their problems without becoming fatigued.

In all these contexts the model of supervision introduced has included creative methods. Jane now shares her reflections on the value of creative supervision and includes a vivid example from her practice.

My decision to take the LCP Creative Supervision Diploma in 2009-10 came out of an interest in grounding my supervision practice and training in a more rigorous understanding of the principles and practices of psychodrama. I had found, myself, that the tools of embodiment, projection and role were personally very powerful and enabled me better to access and process my experiences as a pastor, leader and teacher. They enabled me better to inhabit a love of God and neighbour with my whole heart, soul, mind and strength. Combined with an attention to the narrative and metaphors that are at the heart of religious ways of inhabiting the world I continue to experience these methods as extremely powerful supervision tools.

To illustrate the value of the use of creative methods in the sectors of ministry and education I share an example of a recent supervision with an American colleague of Nigerian origin who works in the University sector. We were working, as we normally do, online.

He began the supervision expressing his dismay at the actions of the President of the United States in the first weeks of 2025 and the consequences for his educational and intercultural work and for the stress levels of so many colleagues, students and clients.

He then went on to describe the chaotic situation in his university role in which two senior colleagues had left the organisation and in which he found himself being pulled in many directions to cover gaps and exceed his level of authority and his capacity.

His objective in supervision was articulated as 'needing to find a way to stand apart from all this chaos'. I invited him to show me what it felt like to be entangled in this chaos – both in the US context and at work. He selected several large cloths and began to whirl them about himself. As the sculpt gained momentum the cloths began to twine around him, and one landed over his head. As he paused to reflect on what was happening, he said, "I am entombed; I am blinded; I cease to exist. I am Lazarus in the tomb".

I asked him what it would take to come out of the tomb. After some thought he removed each cloth and placed it separately at a distance from himself. I asked him if he wanted to address any of these cloths and one by one, he spoke to them, the authority of his own voice growing as he did so.

Once he had deroled the cloths he reflected on how powerful it was to work in this embodied way – both to experience the vortex of the chaos he is living in and the liberation of finding his own voice and power to stand in relation to these forces and create some boundaries and limits for their influence over him. He resolved to speak to his boss about his job description, to limit his consumption of news to certain times of day and to heighten the priority of his own meditation practice.

The embodied way of working released powerful connections for him with the story of the death and resurrection of Lazarus in the Gospel of John in which Jesus calls a man out of the tomb and invites the community to unbind him and let him go, and with the story of Adam naming the animals in the book of Genesis – naming, a part of taming any beast.

For me this example illustrates the potential of creative methods to help supervisees work holistically, drawing on the most powerful images and stories that can help them unlock their own agency and reframe the possibilities of their situations.

We, the three authors of this book, as well as those we have taught, who are practising these methods and approaches, note that there is a by-product to the training. We find our direct practice, whether clinical, educational or creative, is informed and enhanced indirectly but significantly by the integration of these approaches.

As Jane illustrates:

One of the joys of the Supervision Diploma for me was that the medium was the message. We were taught creative supervision through a creative pedagogy. Observing the way in which spaces were created for thinking and learning using the same tools that were offered for supervision has transformed my approach to teaching and to the tasks of leading an educational institution.

Lizzie Palmer, dramatherapist and a recent trainee on the LCP Creative Supervision Training, echoes something of Jane's observations on the broader reaches of this training. Lizzie thinks about these in the context of an individual practitioner. In her concluding self-assessment of the training, she reflects

I feel as though there is much more that I could write about how this course has impacted my self-view and connection to myself both professionally and personally. It has been so important for me to reconnect with this depth of experiential learning and with the trust that I have in myself as a practitioner but also as a person. I have somehow managed to find myself afresh, bringing new value to my clinical experiences and areas of expertise, and to how I trust my instincts and emotions. I feel as though a light has been shone on how others see and experience me in a group, and I am now exploring how to integrate this into how I experience myself.

As her supervisor of supervision, Bryn notes how this is a familiar experience for many trainees. In embarking on a training journey to become a supervisor, the individual carries out a kind of corresponding self-assessment of themselves as a practitioner. This is the base from which they begin. They conduct a personal inventory of their current strengths and weaknesses. This self-assessing perspective continues to evolve throughout the training, reflecting the growth of their internal supervisor function. This notion of the 'inner supervisor' gains real traction when experienced within the structure of a supervisory training. Through the combination of the outer feeding of the training and the resultant inner growth of the supervisor, the associated practitioner role is deeply enriched, reimagined and actualised anew.

References

Ben Kinsella Trust, 2024. *Knife Crime Data for England and Wales* https://benkinsella.org.uk/knife-crime-statistics/ Accessed 9 May 2025.

Haidt, J., 2024. *The Anxious Generation.* Penguin.

Herman, J., 1992. *Trauma and Recovery.* Basic Books.

Leach, J., 2020. *A Charge to Keep: Reflective Supervision and the Renewal of Christian Leadership.* Foundry Press.

Methodist Conference Past Cases Review, 2015. https://media.methodist.org.uk/media/documents/past-cases-review-2013-2015-final_gX8C3IL.pdf Accessed 22 May 2025.

Methodist Conference Supervision Report, 2017. https://media.methodist.org.uk/media/documents/counc-mc17-46-supervision-april-2017_DN49zD0.pdf Accessed 22 May 2025

Methodist Conference Reflective Supervision Report, 2021. www.pastoralsupervision.org.uk. Accessed 22 May 2025.

Office for National Statistics, 2024. *Crime in England and Wales: Police Force Area data tables.* www.ons.gov.uk/peoplepopulationandcommunity/crimeandjustice/bulletins/crimeinenglandandwales/yearendingdecember2024. Accessed 5 November 2025.

The Observer, 2024. *Toxic Online Culture Fuelling Rise in Sexual Assaults on Children by Other Children, Police Warn.* www.theguardian.com/society/2024/feb/17/toxic-online-culture-fuelling-rise-in-sexual-assualts-on-children-by-other-children-police-warn Accessed 9 May 2025.

Chapter 13

Creative Supervision with.in the Outdoors

Céline Butté and Bryn Jones

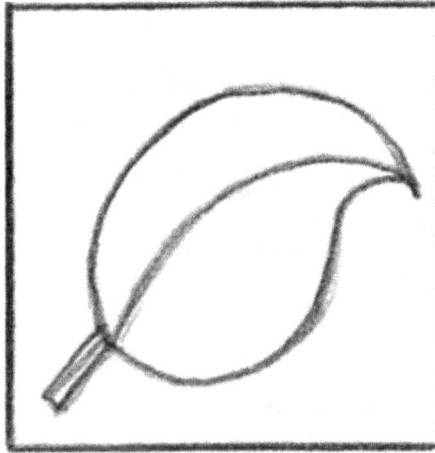

Figure 13.0

This chapter holds a different point of focus compared to the others contained within this volume. It outlines an approach rather than a specific method. It is also distinct in that it does not describe a technique which is currently taught on the LCP Creative Supervision Diploma training. Instead, in writing the chapter we have followed a methodology that matches the nature and rhythm of supervising outdoors. In this we as authors follow and are guided by the contours of our unfolding inquiry in ways similar to the supervisee who is enabled to reflect upon practice guided by prompts from the natural environment and the active and dialogic presence of their supervisor. Such approaches tend more towards a circumambulatory style rather than a direct and linear form. This way of working and the described approach to supervising outdoors is a live and developing practice interest for us both. Exploring this here marks an important acknowledgement of the new and emergent ways supervision is being developed and delivered. It also reflects the laboratory-type approach we employ in the development of new creative methods

DOI: 10.4324/9781003435655-17

which may become part of the training in future years. Providing an insight into one such approach, the writing takes a critical look at how the clarity and containment of the supervisory space might be preserved in different settings.

The spelling 'with.in' in the chapter title invites a pause to recognise that this neologism is in fact key to what we are articulating here. Indeed, the immersive and relational element so simply contained in this preposition is what becomes the bedrock of the work. As psychotherapist and geologist, Ruth Allen so clearly states:

> *Words to describe a practice can get in the way of a nuanced understanding of what the work is really about, especially when they become buzzwords or 'mainstreamed' to the degree that they lose their heart. For example, 'nature', 'nature connection' and 'outdoors' – what do we mean by these terms? Is nature just 'green and outside' or is it also what is most essentially human? What is the value of 'outside' if it serves as nothing more than a backdrop? How does 'outdoor' obscure or subvert an intended ethic of deep, intertwined relationality behind a blunt methodological term? As I mature in my 'outdoor practice' I recognise that it is easy to bracket what outdoor means and foreclose a variety of possibilities of how to work, and what needs to be tended to. I am less invested in being outside these days, than capturing an ethic of 'outdoors' which centres relationality across ecologies and ecosystems, a deep consideration of the systems and 'field' of a client and therapist's lives, and what it means to be the human animal in a heating, dying world. This is bringing me into a much deeper alignment with my ecological underpinnings.*
>
> (supervisory conversation, 25.5.25)

Movement and therefore action are inherent to working with.in the outdoors. This contrasts with the creative methods presented in Part II whereby supervisor and supervisee both initially sit in their respective chairs ahead of transitioning into action by way of the creative method. In fact, we would suggest that working with.in the outdoors *is* the action method.

The chapter follows four pathways.

- The Emerging Path – what has led us to work outdoors; our relevant background, prior practice experience and interests in outdoor work.
- The Conversing Path – an outdoor conversation about this approach recorded on a walk together through ancient woodland
- The Reflecting Path – reflections from supervisees the authors have worked with in outdoor contexts
- The Practical Path – our subsequent thoughts and onward considerations for supervisory practice outdoors

The Emerging Path

What has led us to work outdoors; our relevant background, prior practice experience and interests in outdoor work

Bryn

Over recent years and especially during the global COVID-19 pandemic, I have developed my therapeutic and supervisory practice beyond the four walls of the consulting room. The years of the pandemic, social distancing and lock down provided a prompt for many to consider new ways of practising including working online and outdoors. This was certainly a factor in the evolution of my own practice. Additionally, I have become aware that there are deeper roots informing and shaping my own interest. These stretch further back, and it is striking to acknowledge how they underpin my more recently developed practice of working outdoors in a supervisory context.

In considering where these recent practice interests and developments might be founded, I was surprised to discover a substantial and coherent lineage of interrelated practice. This within itself reminds me of how valuable it can be to pause and glance over one's own shoulder, to look again from where we came. Only in seeing from this entirely new perspective of the present, am I able to identify the individual markers which connect up to form a continual line.

The first and most distant of these reflections takes me back to childhood. I recall playing in solitude whilst staying with my grandparents in rural Wales. I would nestle myself against the foot of a tree, one in a long row of old, old yew trees which lined up alongside a stream. Sat in their shade, on a soft cushioned floor of fallen pine needles I would play. My only toys, the natural bits and pieces I might find lying around; stones, twigs, leaves and branches. These I would gather and combine, bend and snap and cluster and scatter, in ways which helped make some kind of sense of the predicaments, joys and pains of my young life.

Fast forwarding from there to more recent examples located in professional practice contexts, I identified several salient examples. As a creative facilitator, I devised and directed participatory creative programmes in the outdoors for various groups. These aimed to enable responsive engagement with the natural environment through play, story-making and art-making and towards identifying and articulating aspects of oneself as reflected in elements of the immediate environment, streams, trees, leaves, sunlight and shadow. As a theatre maker, I directed a series of theatrical audio-driven walking journeys which took Charles Dickens' collection of insomnia-fuelled essays *The Uncommercial Traveller* (Dickens 2015) as their starting point. These pieces delved into the shadowy urban underbelly of their city locations to excavate the hidden and untold stories of walkways, underpasses, abandoned shops and lonely street corners. The performances combined story, place, active touch and soundscape to create intimate, sensory adventures.

These projects have come to form my pathway to working outdoors. They have fostered in me an openness, a porousness and a curiosity around the differences we come to feel *within* through identifying symbolic and representational aspects of ourselves *without*. This prior practice lineage has informed my understanding of how the external environment might evoke, resonate and release aspects of one's inner world which might otherwise remain unseen, unspoken or unrealised. It is this creative and productive encounter between outer and inner that intrigues me and underscores my subsequent practice in taking therapy and supervision outdoors.

Céline

My outdoor supervision and consultation practice with individuals and small groups often includes some time in the studio. Sessions may last longer than the conventional 50-minute hour, sometimes stretching over a full day to two-day intensives, which provides the space to delve into the timelessness that often comes with being outdoors. As I track back to the possible origins of this way of working, I too find a unique and personal lineage that interweaves a long-standing search for relationality within my dance movement and therapy practice.

I grew up in a small hamlet in the depths of rural Normandy, our house surrounded by farmland and a humble farming culture all around. Everyone was always busy on the farms it seemed. I often felt lonely and overwhelmed by the absence of the other. In contrast, my imagination and experiments with balance and gravity outdoors on my trapeze were reliable and safe places to retreat to.

My family culture celebrated creativity. Joining a circus school at the age of five instilled in me the value never to take myself too seriously and the importance of attention to detail. As a professional dancer, I took part in several site-specific physical theatre performances in the UK and abroad, initiatives that spoke to a long-standing inquiry into what defines a stage and how to reach broader audiences. Since qualifying as a DMP, my practice has been further enriched by a colourful palette of outdoors and studio-based projects that continue to shape my work and research (Butté, 2023). Move into Life workshops with Sandra Reeve, movement artist, dance movement psychotherapist and graduate of the LCP Creative Supervision Diploma, opened my body and mind to ecological movement practice in natural settings. Training in Body Mind Centering® and delving more deeply into the matter that we are made of, the living body, has offered profound healing and made my inner landscape a source of endless fascination. The aRTSjAM, a collective of arts therapists I co-created and have belonged to for over 10 years (Bent et al., 2026), has enabled me to experiment, release and reflect with colleagues, through improvised dance movement, music and mark-making, in both studios and outdoors. More recently, during COVID-19, I joined an introductory training to Ecological Transactional Analysis (Eco-TA) with Hayley Marshall and Giles Barrow, who became guides to anchoring my clinical practice in local woodland. There was time online and time outdoors, an extraordinary combination so typical of the COVID-19 years.

There is something I find particularly complementary when time is spent in the studio, where one might be less inhibited with improvised dance movement, more contained maybe by the four walls, and time spent outdoors. The time spent in the studio may be experienced as a warmup for the moving-dancing body as well as an opportunity to identify a supervisory question or theme, whilst the time spent outdoors opens up the opportunity to be with an inquiry immersed with.in a less predictable and more enlivened environment.

We invite you to pause here and to reflect upon your own history and experience of play, discovery and exploration in the outdoors. Connect with these lineages and notice how they might feed your interest in ways both personal and unique, relational and communal.

The Conversing Path

An outdoor conversation about this approach recorded on a walk together through ancient woodland

This is a lightly edited transcript of our walk whereby we reflect on our individual practitioner experience of supervising outdoors. The conversation, like a walk-through woodland, is far ranging and often taken by unplanned paths of interest and serendipitous moments. In refraining from over-editing the writing, we hope the reader is able to gain a tangible sense of outdoor work in ways both practical and encouraging.

Bryn: We have planned to meet at a gateway to the woods on a Friday morning in April. Spring has sprung. The sky is blue. Many of the trees are in budburst with some beginning to leaf out. This freshening sense of new emergence feels fitting and chimes with the nature of the chapter we are hoping to write. I sit on the gate waiting for Céline to arrive. I'm sitting at a threshold, behind me a tranche of ancient woodland, habitat for flora and fauna long established on this hillside. Ahead of me, a massive new housing development rises to provide new homes for newcomers. I'm put in touch with notions of encroachment, another kind of emergence. This one is driven by the very real-world housing needs of our overflowing cities; the challenges of preservation and the hope for spaces which can be shared. Suddenly Céline arrives, not in front of me, as I was expecting but from behind, having entered the woods via another path. I'm immediately put in touch with the often unplanned and serendipitous nature of working outdoors!

Céline: I am all set: location in phone, journey planned and plenty of time to get to our agreed meeting point. There is no traffic on the roads on this peaceful, sunny day. I feel light and excited at the prospect of sharing our practice outdoors in these ancient woodlands which Bryn is familiar with and that I also have a connection to from the past. When I get to the station, however, my journey takes a different turn. My train and all subsequent trains have been cancelled. It takes me some time to find my bearings and finally decide to catch a taxi. I will be late, I inform Bryn. The taxi eventually stops in an estate, at the edge of the woodlands. I realise that this entrance into the woods is not the one we had planned. Close enough, I carry on from here on foot, through the woods. As I walk up the path, my senses immediately extend out. The uneven ground underfoot, the many shades of green and brown all around, the curves and windy lines, the sound of birds close by and urban life further away, the smell of the soil. I breathe. I am walking fast as I do not want to be delayed any longer than necessary, but I am more fully present, nearly there, arriving more with every step; amused even at the thought that I will arrive late, but from within the woods.

Bryn: So, we have arrived here Céline and the varying ways we have done so puts me in touch with this notion of 'the getting to' when working outdoors. It seems an important point of consideration. How and when and from where is our supervisee going to arrive? Our attention to this as being *part of* the work seems necessary and significant. Now there is the question of how from the meeting point, do we approach the site within which we might work? At this point, I look to guide my supervisee into a kind of preamble. This can be an important ritual marker in outdoor work. In this there is the defining of a preliminary space that incorporates a threshold and enables a kind of moving 'away from' and 'moving into'. This is what the ethnographer and folklorist van Gennep might refer to as the 'preliminary stage' (van Gennep, 1960: 10) from his 'Rites de Passage' schema. This symbolic act helps an individual separate themselves from any limiting or overbearing social, professional or cultural context and to mark the beginning of a transitional process (see Chapter 2 on warmup).

Céline: This makes me think about expectations when working with practitioners who have not worked outdoors before and who may need support to orient themselves. There might be anticipatory questions. There is also my curiosity as I orient to this specific person or group: *'Will they move in the shade or in a more sunny and exposed part of the landscape?'* As they pause in a location of their choice, supervisees have the time to focus on the question or theme that they have brought or refined earlier in the studio. Whilst respecting the environment, they may create something with objects available to them or develop a piece of dance-movement.

Bryn: Those initial and apparently urgent questions you mention are familiar, aren't they? The 'what now?' of the work. These woods, which I work in, have a gently inclining pathway which I use for the preamble or warmup and as a space for those anxious 'What now?' concerns to be named and held. The path runs from an unremarkable and easily missed gateway. The gateway opens from the inside edge of a pavement which hugs a busy road. To pass through the gate is to traverse a threshold. One which leads from the clatter and glare of the everyday to a shadier place of quietude.

After just a couple of initial steps down the path, supervisees will often remark; "ahh ... that's better ... Wow, it's suddenly so quiet ... This feels like Narnia!" The utterance of these innocent phrases marks a palpable shift. A movement from 'what was' to 'what is'. It is often the case that they arrive with the accumulation of their day. In this way the preamble facilitates a kind of decompression process. I attempt to join and support them in this. I nod to acknowledge their take on the differences they notice. As we walk on, I just hold space for the transition to gather and settle. The sound of the road fades step by step. The tree cover and foliage thicken. The expansive woodland ahead comes into view. Somewhere along this path I will invite a supervisory question; 'What are you bringing to think about and explore today?' We talk as we walk, exploring the question and hopefully by the preliminary path's end, it is complete and clear enough to steer or inform the subsequent steps of the inquiry.

Céline: This reminds me of Sandra Reeve who talks about ecological movement and the ecological body (Reeve, 2011) and stresses this remarkable point: stopping comes in the line of movement not the other way around.

An ecological body is situated in flux, participation and change. The changing body/soma experienced through movement as part of the changing environment challenges any fixed and deterministic notion of self and stimulates a different sense of self as process, participating in the movement of life.

(Reeve, 2011: 51)

We do not start from stopping, we are moving and then we stop. But even when we 'stop', a lot of micro- and internal movement is still going on. Being outdoors brings this principle back to the surface and maybe challenges the more conventional idea of 'arriving' in supervision: it places it at a transitory threshold rather than in that moment when both supervisor and supervisee(s) sit down in their respective chairs in the consulting room. As we walk and scout the area together with supervisees, we are on the go. Maybe this movement feeds a sense that we are going somewhere to a (predetermined) destination. Supervisees may also have questions about the history of the place; how do we, as supervisors, engage with these curiosities? supporting supervisees to locate themselves in the place and know a little about the landscape, so that they make more informed choices about where to go next. Or do we leave the mystery, inviting them to work more intuitively? I am remembering a time when I worked with a group in an unfamiliar location. Part of our arriving ritual was to go on a recce together so that not only they, but I could find my bearings and demarcate with the group the territory that we would cover. We agreed to not go beyond a line recognisable by specific changes on the ground or in the landscape. This boundary contained our group.

Bryn: Yes, that links to another important consideration in how we ensure the safety of supervision practice outdoors. In making this offer to step outside, it is incumbent upon us as supervisors to ensure that we can confidently guide and safely care for our supervisees. Practically, and as you mentioned earlier, it is important that we are well accustomed with the site. I visit and recce these woods regularly. I am familiar with the twists and turns of the land. I know the various potential paths that might be followed. I am mindful of seasonal changes and weather conditions and ready to advise the cancellation of a session if these threaten personal safety. In saying this, I am also keen to avoid falling into a 'fair weather' approach to outdoor work. It is often through encountering sudden turns in the weather, seasonal shifts and changing climatic conditions that an especially immediate and visceral supervisory insight arises. However, this requires consideration on the side of general safety as well as the individual capacities and preferences of the supervisee.

Céline: I hold in mind the importance of choosing paths that allow for two people to walk side-by-side rather than one in front of the other. It is a practical consideration that offers choice and supports reciprocity.

Bryn: In the first session outdoors, I explain that there is a round walk which we can comfortably complete within the time we have available. However, I will also say that there is licence to wander, pause, and meander. I want to be clear that there is no expectation or need to complete that round walk. Simply, that it is there if wished for. This seems to land and be understood as it is rarely the case that an entire circum-ambulation of the round walk is ever completed. We are invariably and wondrously diverted! It seems that at some point, something else will happen; a pause point, a reflection or immersion which is evoked by the landscape. Suddenly we are in this emergent space with our supervisee and alive to what might be taking shape. An unplanned moment suddenly constellates, and we are actually stopped by nature. The inquiry is pulled into focus by something discovered within or through the environment. A connection is forged and that which was previously unseen or unthought surfaces and quite literally, stops us in our tracks.

Céline: And that is the beauty of it: there are more of these opportunities outside than in the studio. I remember a supervisee sitting at the base of a tree and sharing how this outdoor location suddenly caused her to recall the potential members of a new therapy group she had been wanting to set up. She described the value in having the time and space to be reminded of this plan and to sit and consider each of the potential participants in turn. Through this moment a supervisory question came into focus and my distinct supervisory role was clarified. More broadly, I am now thinking, how do we attend to the five roles of the supervisor in outdoor settings?

Bryn: These responsibilities rest with the supervisor; to assess the outdoor site, to be clear in delineating and working within time boundaries and to attend to safety. This is an example of the supervisor as both administrator and evaluator (see Chapter 3). Then, as the process begins, there is a shift as the supervisor moves into a more facilitative role. When introducing a supervisee to working outdoors, I am in the role of supervisor as facilitator. There is an extra dimension to the facilitator role when outdoors that has something of the quality of an outdoor guide. I hold the responsibility of somebody who, to some degree, knows this path, knows this landscape and who is prepared for a number of eventualities that might play out. I ready myself to make further calls on the side of safety, containment or practicality. As the journey unfolds the role, responsibility and skill of the Guide is to track the outdoor supervisory process in supportive, adaptive, containing and yet unobtrusive ways. It is by holding these considerations in mind that we are able to locate ourselves clearly within the appropriate supervisory role when working outdoors.

Céline: Thinking about the other two supervisory roles, walking or moving together outdoors lends itself to the consultant role, as I share in dialogue from my own experience. As for the role of supervisor as educator, in the way that I work, this seems to appear more often when we are back in the studio and reflecting back on the session as a whole.

Bryn: I'm struck that as we walk here today, the other people who pass by all appear to be here for a particular purpose; running to keep fit or walking a dog. Nobody seems to be just out for a wander. It's making me reflect on the nature of walking and how the notion of going for a walk and one's relationship with the environment can be conditioned by many things, including gender. Historically we all inherit these images, usually of men or more specifically those 'gentlemen explorers' heroically adventuring and conquering; attempting to go higher or further or 'discover' or in pursuit of material gain. All of this is imbued with some form of supposed 'noble' purpose, which usually turns out to be inflated or exploitative or in the case of colonialism, both. In supervising outdoors, it seems important to be mindful of these unconscious imperatives and to wonder how an alternative, a counteroffer might be made? It seems clear to me that a more open, reciprocal and responsive way of journeying is more effective and of greater value. I don't look to enforce this in a prescriptive or demanding way. It is important I think to allow people to arrive as they are and start from where they are. However, I do hold in mind, perhaps on their behalf, the right to roam and wander and to become porous in the face of the environment so that it might prompt, evoke or reflect a new thought, feeling or insight. It is through establishing a discourse between oneself and the environment that meaning might form and a non-preconceived purpose might constellate. It is through awe, surprise, wonder and reverie that this approach finds its validation. This is making me think of the 'feminine sublime' which I learnt about through the writings of Ursula Le Guin (Le Guin, 1981). According to Le Guin, this is the embodiment of a different kind of power and being, one characterised not by physical strength or dominance but by intuition, empathy and a connection to nature and the natural world.

Céline: Yes, we can only get to that reciprocity if we tap into a sense of receptivity within. In contrast, if we are passing through a particular piece of land or woodland with a destination in mind, such as when I was walking uphill on my way to meet you today, we are not going to stop.

Bryn: In thinking about the evocative nature of working outdoors and aligned with the powerful role of the reciprocal that we have been discussing, it seems important to be attentive to how we sustain the supervisory focus and orientation of the work. How do we look after the frame, ensuring it remains a reflection on practice rather than a personal process? I think acknowledging that there may often be a call to the supervisory domain of Eye 8 (see chapter 3) is helpful. So, we can make space for more immediate and personalised responses but in ways which retain a supervisory focus.

Céline: A supervisee once described how without the holding of working outdoors, she would not have been able to navigate her way through previously constructed ways of being and old behavioural patterns that no longer served her or her practice. She spoke of the way she met the land, and the land met her during outdoor supervision sessions. As supervisor, this put me in touch with notions of my own role in guiding, witnessing and holding this piece of work, alongside the natural elements and together in service of her practice.

Bryn: There are times in guiding or facilitating outdoor work, that I do find myself taking a more direct role. For example, sometimes as part of the preamble, I will suggest we walk in silence. I frame it as an invitation to make a connection with this place, the woods and to come into presence and be aware of it around us. To hear for instance, that wood pigeon who has just called from within the woods and who would otherwise have likely gone unheard and unnoticed. I do think that at times, this needs to be facilitated otherwise it won't naturally occur.

Céline: Working outdoors offers a multitude of sensory experiences that invite us to be more in the moment. The immediacy and potency of tuning into our senses brings us home to our body which may be welcome for some and a relief, but it might also be quite unsettling.

Bryn: That there are also political elements associated with working outdoors seems an inescapable aspect of such practice. And I would say, increasingly so. I think it begins to announce itself through the disconnect that so many feel with the natural environment. It is becoming normalised for ever greater numbers of people to have little or no experience of just being in and spending time in the natural environment. So, when people do step in and when we open up work in woodland, a political element may also surface. Only in coming back to such spaces, might they notice how quiet and refreshing it can feel and how unavailable spaces like this might have become for them. So, we are put in touch with the ways land is owned and managed and how access to it is prioritised and controlled. We work against the backdrop of the staggering fact that in the United Kingdom by law of trespass, we are excluded from 92% of the land and 97% of its waterways. (Hayes, 2021: 13–19)

Céline: Where are we intending to practice, who do we seek permission from? For example, for my work outdoors I completed a Park User Agreement with my local authority and was advised to contact the Friends of the Woodlands I wanted to practice within. We are talking about practising supervision in a natural environment; What right do we have to this particular location, to all this space? Each place has a history, its own community and guardians; how do we connect with these in order to maybe nurture a sense of mutual respect and belonging rather than usurping and becoming a potential threat as strangers to the land?

Bryn: I am put in touch with a particular memory as you mention requesting permission from the 'guardians of the place'. There is a prosaic, literal and legal aspect to such requests but it's also taking me back to land-based projects I was involved with in Malaysia. There, ahead of us beginning our work, colleagues would propitiate and make offerings to local guardian spirits known as *Datuk Keramat*. Such acts convey a respectful attitude of humility and acknowledgement towards the spiritual and natural ancestry of the land upon and within which we are temporary visitors. This seems to me a helpful consideration which can support us in finding our own culturally relevant ways to mindfully locate ourselves within the natural environment.

Céline: Yes, as we entered the woods a moment ago, we had to stop at the oak trees; it felt as if we were greeting them as you shared part of the recent stories of the local community getting together to save them. In fact, it might even have been these ancient trees themselves who mobilised the local community to save them through the invisible rhizomatic network of the land. The story that comes with a place is powerful.

Bryn: Another consideration in choosing to work outdoors is to recognise that it isn't any kind of universal panacea that works for all! There are many important considerations here about assessing the interest and readiness of an individual to meaningfully engage with a process such as supervisory work outdoors. It is important to contain and process our own enthusiasm and/or our potentially shadowy drives for working outdoors. What is the appeal to us? Are we looking to escape the humdrum of the consulting room or looking to reinvigorate our practice with something new and vital? So, we need to think about how we approach this possibility. How might we contract and negotiate the idea with a supervisee and in ways which recognise that it might be a productive process for someone for some of the time but not necessarily for everybody, all of the time.

Céline: I am now thinking about time. How do we set and manage the pace of the work. Working outdoors, I tune in to my supervisee's rhythm in order to anticipate and calibrate the time ahead the best I can, so that we return to our starting point in good time. Time dissolves when working in the natural environment, we fall into timeless time – Kairos (open endedness). Chronos (the ticking of clock time) (Negueruela-Azarola, 2025) is another of the supervisor's responsibilities and can be harder to keep hold of. This is not entirely surprising. Outdoor locations such as these ancient woodlands are infused with a different relationship to time. Maybe working outdoors takes us right back to a more visceral, internal clock?

Bryn: Yes, okay so as an example of Kairos; right now, I am taken by that little sapling over there with those very pale green leaves. Just there underneath that tree and those fresh leaves are completely caught in the sunlight. Everything else is totally still but they are alive like a flame, like a tiny green flame dancing.

Céline: You are noticing something visual whilst I am drawn to the sounds around, the birds and the sound of machines in the neighbourhood. But this is the sensory stimulation I am talking about, whether it is what we see, what we hear, what we touch, what we smell or maybe even what we taste, working outdoors awakens the senses.

Bryn: In our consciously choosing to work outdoors as a supervisor, we are authentically modelling a belief in this approach as a valid, productive and purposeful process. We are not simply replaying a flat formulaic exercise but actually stepping into a live and dynamic unfolding process. In this, we are declaring that this is an approach that we are investing in and exploring as a practitioner.

Céline: Therese O'Driscoll, who coined the term eco-supervisor, describes her approach as embodied, embedded, emergence. She explains:

This openness to receiving and becoming aware of all that is around us whilst being received by earth, wind, flower, stream or place is pivotal to Eco Supervision. This is the supervisee-supervisor-environment triadic system in motion.

(O'Driscoll, 2023: 55)

Bryn: Over recent years there has been a growing awareness and appreciation of being in nature, engaging with the natural world and various forms of outdoor work. This has led to an ever-expanding evidence base cohering itself around such practices. We know well, how through the act of walking; thinking, imagining and envisioning prospers. The countless ways the step-by-step mobilisation of the body through space can support creativity, free flow ideas, reduce stress and improve cognitive functioning. It seems to me that all of this is further enhanced when done in certain sensorial environments, such as woodland, whereby all the senses are simultaneously enlivened. It then fosters a kind of *thinking – sensing – feeling* dialogue loop which can be exceptionally enriching.

Céline: Yes, the outdoors is a sensory connective place and here we are, pausing as we arrive back to where we had started, getting ready to leave. There is often a natural turn to the conversation when my supervisee and I recognise that we are getting closer to the place where we had originally met. Sometimes there is a pause, not far from this original threshold. This moment of punctuation enables us both to acknowledge the end of the session and make way for closing reflections where they may share what they are taking from the session or consider next steps.

The Reflecting Path

Reflections from Davina Holmes, a supervisee one of the authors has worked with in outdoor contexts.

I have found my Supervision in Nature sessions to be calming, restorative and revelatory, moving through ancient woodland with my supervisor Bryn alongside me. Exploring different paths and natural formations shaped by the seasons has allowed me to experience nature as a giant 'projector' of my practice. The ever-changing environment has clarified and reflected various aspects of my practice that require consideration, change and development. In the brief writings below, I chart the progressive narrative of my supervision sessions, the elements of practice that were explored by the changing seasons through Winter and into Spring.

Winter

I am experiencing compassion fatigue, in both my personal and professional life. Of all the trees in this ancient forest, I choose a tree that is not native. A Cedar of Lebanon. I am not native either, yet I belong to this land ancestrally through my English parents. Later reading about the Cedar of Lebanon, I discover the symbolic importance of this tree and its ability to withstand storms, contrasting seasons, destruction, drought and to extend its roots even within the hardest terrain.

Yet on this day the tallest tree has not managed to weather the storm intact and one of its large branches has fallen to the ground. The smell of the inner wood is fresh and laid bare. My supervisor introduces me to the concept of pollarding, suggesting that although painful for the tree, this natural act of pollarding could release weight from its branches to allow it to grow more effectively towards the light.

I am a tall tree
In an ancient forest
I am strong
My trunk is resilient from many storms
Imprinted in my roots burrowed deep
My branches reach up to the sky
Far and wide
Supporting and sheltering
I am a strong canopy
For many others
And yet
Last night's storm was one too many
I could no longer hold such weight
My left limb wrenched from its socket
Exposes flesh
Parts of my Self
Lying on the forest floor
Wounded
Fresh with the smell of pain
I am a tall tree
In an ancient forest
And yet
I am vulnerable

Reflecting creatively on this experience encountered through outdoor supervision, took me back to a painful memory of a shoulder injury. This resulted in me 'pollarding' some of my work. It led me into a natural process, stepping away from being a therapist and developing my work as a supervisor. The injury made me confront my physical vulnerability, the limits of my ongoing emotional capacity to work with children and to trust in my new growth as a supervisor.

Winter 2

I stumble upon an old tree which has fallen in the night, blocking our path. I am struck by the entanglement of ivy clinging to it and I feel a sense that the tree is being choked by the ivy. Moving away from the tree, I start to consider what this might be reflecting back to me. I start to speak about painful experiences regarding racial conflict, defensiveness and avoidance within one of the teams I supervise. I have been attempting to hold a neutral role yet now I realise how entangled I am. I recognise a clinginess to maintain a sense of belonging within the team.

With my supervisor's support, I start to consider ways of disentangling myself from some of the relationships I have within the team. I begin to see my own role more clearly. Instead of expecting myself to support everyone, I signpost them to people outside of the setting who they can reach out to. In doing so, I refer on work to other practitioners and feel less attached to the loss of money from doing so. As a result, I gain clarity around my purpose and feel less constricted in my practice.

Spring

Today we choose another path and discover a circle of trees which I walk through and continue. I turn and suddenly laugh as I stumble across yet another fallen tree. This one has been caught by other trees as it fell. I climb along its trunk, balancing and feeling child-like, yet I don't want to stay. I continue again along the path, stopping by a tree which appears to stand alone. This one is heavy-laden with ivy. It seems to lean under the weight. There are no other trees nearby to catch it, should it fall. I suddenly feel tearful and overwhelmed. I turn away. I don't want to be that tree.

My supervisor stands with me, and I share my concerns for the tree bearing such a load in isolation. I look back to the fallen tree and notice that the trees it is surrounded by are trees of the same species, oak trees. *I come to talk of the joy of other work with arts therapists, recognising the need to be working with others and the risk involved in continually working alone.*

Davina Holmes
Dance Movement Psychotherapist and Supervisor

The Practical Path

Our subsequent thoughts and onward considerations for supervisory practice outdoors

As Bryn and I each take time to revisit the recording of our conversation in the woods, we notice three particular terms that speak to a possible emerging methodology for supervision with.in the outdoors, clarifying something that pertains to the emergent and nourishing aspects of both being outdoors and being in movement – moving with the body of the earth whilst inhabiting our earthbody and to the logistical sides of this approach to supervision.

As supervisors working with.in the outdoors, we note an immediate awakening of a multifaceted *receptive capacity*. This includes our receptivity to what our supervisee brings, as per our work in the clinic or studio but also our receptivity to what the practice location presents us with. To this, we must *respond* in a way that attends to maintaining safe practice and our contract with supervisees, that is, attending to the conversation and creative work outdoors in such a way that the supervisory theme or question is always in sight or certainly within easy reach. Finally, practicing with.in the outdoors is an ecological undertaking. Sessions take place in an environment that carries themes of life and death as well as cyclical and seasonal changes. We are immediately touched by that which we encounter, and we also impact the environment by our presence. This *reciprocity* is the salient edge of a practice with.in the outdoors.

On this, the final path of our chapter, we revisit and draw from the above to compile a formative checklist of considerations for those interested in exploring supervision outdoors. The list is by no means definitive but acts as a guide rooted in our own research and practice. This is fed and supplemented by the wise insights of others who have tread such paths more thoroughly than ourselves. We speak back to some of what we discuss on the Conversing Path. We also share a short list of suggested further reading.

Why Supervise Outdoors?

As we found when asking ourselves this question, you may find that working outdoors has developed naturally as a characteristic of your practice. It may be that you have a positive personal experience of outdoor work or are looking to revitalise and expand the horizons of your current practice. In any case, we recommend that this primary question is given sufficient attention and consideration. It is a significant step and, as such, brings significant potential consequences. It will be helpful to approach the question gradually, to raise and explore it in your own supervision and therapy, discuss the idea with trusted colleagues and thereby build a sound foundation for new practice.

Personal Preparation and Identification of a Suitable Site

Once a clear decision to develop your practice in this way is made, you may look to enrol on suitable CPD training opportunities, conduct your own literature review of the field and begin to identify and familiarise yourself with a suitable site. There are a growing number of training courses in ecotherapy/ecopsychology and we have provided some suggested further reading below.

The identification of a suitable site is a key aspect. This needs to be clearly assessed in several ways including risk, safety, access and aesthetics. The responsibility of guiding a supervisee into an otherwise unknown terrain is considerable. It is imperative that you spend sufficient time walking the site, at differing times of day, preferably across different seasons and at regular intervals throughout the year. You should aim to build up a thorough, experiential working knowledge of the live environment. This will support you in discussing, assessing and contracting the work with your supervisee.

The site itself need not conform to conventional notions of natural beauty, rural idyll nor hold any sense of being a 'special place'. It is enough that it is outdoor. It may be parkland, hinterland, urban or rural. It is good preparatory practice to imagine what the site offers aesthetically and creatively and to be alive to what new or more or different it might offer a supervisee. However, in saying this avoid any moves to control or condition your supervisee's individual experience and interpretation of the site. Refrain from anticipating their responses. Be open to be surprised at what new discoveries they make and how through them you too may discover the site anew.

Insurance and First Aid

You will need to discuss with your insurers how to enhance your professional/ public liability insurance to cover working outdoors. In the case of there being an accident during outdoor work, you become the first responder. It is recommended that you look to enrol on an outdoor first aid training course and that you put together a small first aid kit to be carried with you when working outdoors. You will need to always carry a phone with you, so you are able to call for assistance if necessary.

Assessment

Time spent on a carefully considered assessment of when, why and for whom outdoor supervision is suitable is recommended.

The question of what and who initiates a move to outdoor work seems especially significant. It is becoming increasingly common for people we work with to be open to or actively seeking work outdoors. They may have read an article about the benefits of nature-based inquiry. In this the supervisor is able to respond to existent interest, facilitate a reflective process, review options and negotiate a suitable way forward. There may be occasions when from the side of the supervisor or the supervisee, an idea to work outdoors is a response to a flatness in the current supervisory process or relationship. This requires a clearer analysis so as to avoid the risk of an unconscious escape into novelty. A murky beginning such as this will likely fail to enrich the supervisory process or sustain the supervisory relationship. Particular care is needed should the initial suggestion be made by the supervisor. In this the supervisee may experience the idea as a judgement on the existent work as being ineffective or inadequate.

As in all supervisory work, the process appears to prosper when the inquiry is truly collaborative. This can be aided by outdoor work. In being outdoors together, a shift occurs in the power dynamics between supervisor and supervisee. Look to utilise this towards the establishment of a balanced, reciprocal and transparent dialogue with your supervisee, one able to visit the cons as well as the pros of working outdoors. There is invariably the excitement that comes with doing something differently. This can be useful fuel to support change, but we should know it will burn up swiftly. Look to bring rigour to the decision-making and aim to agree a meaningful, realistic and sustainable way forward.

> When you give yourself to places, they give you yourself back; the more one comes to know them, the more one seeds them with the invisible crop of memories and associations that will be waiting for you when you come back, while new places offer up new thoughts, new possibilities. Exploring the world is one of the best ways of exploring the mind and walking travels both terrains.
>
> (Solnit, 2001: 111)

Contracting and Boundaries

As indicated above, clear assessments of the site, the individual and the supervisory purpose are key first steps. This enables you and your supervisee to begin forming an agreement. Look to clarify if this new arrangement is to be trialled initially and if so what is the time-line for this to be reviewed? If the move to working outdoors involves the development of already existent work, an acknowledgement of the impact on the supervisory frame will be helpful.

Several boundaries need to be considered including confidentiality, timing and weather conditions. Confidentiality is affected as the space you now work in is public. What are the agreed protocols for encountering other people, some of whom may on occasion be known to you or your supervisee? How will you orientate yourselves around encounters with dogs, school trips and sudden changes in the weather? In considering timings, look to establish clear markers that help clarify when, where and how the session begins and ends.

Weather becomes another live and uncontrollable feature when working outdoors. Explore with your supervisee their own weather preferences and capacities. Support them to think through what needs they may have and advise them in preparing suitable clothing and footwear for the site and season. It is also advisable to include a cancellation/alternative venue clause in the case of inclement weather, apparent injury or personal limitation and an agreement that you as supervisor hold the 'right to decide' on the side of safety.

Remember to check for any legal land-use restrictions placed on the site you wish to work in. There are some apparently public sites that still require permission for access and use.

In working outdoors, the natural environment itself becomes the container for the work. It may also prompt the content and focus of the work and provide the materials for the creative exploration of what is being examined. Recognising and allowing the outdoors to inform, guide and become part of the work is an essential element in developing progressive and purposeful supervisory work outdoors.

Suggested Further Reading

Atkins, S., and Snyder, M., 2017. *Nature-Based Expressive Arts Therapy: Integrating the Expressive Arts and Ecotherapy*. Jessica Kingsley Publishers.

Jordan, M., 2014. *Nature and Therapy: Understanding counselling and psychotherapy in outdoor spaces*. Routledge.

Jordan, M., and Marshall, H., 2010. "Taking Counselling and Psychotherapy Outside: Destruction or Enrichment of the Therapeutic Frame?" *European Journal of Psychotherapy and Counselling*, *12*(4), pp. 345–359.

Kaplan, R., and Kaplan, S., 1989. *The Experience of Nature: A psychological perspective*. Cambridge University Press.

Siddons Heginworth, I., 2009. *Environmental Art Therapy and the Tree of Life*. Spirit's Rest Publications.

Solnit, R., 2017. *A Field Guide to Getting Lost*. Canongate.

Solnit, R., 2025. *No Straight Road Takes You There: Essays for Uneven Terrain*. Granta.

Wilson, L., 2022. *Sites of Transformation*. Bloomsbury.

References

Bent, C., Butté, C. Rova, M. Unkovich, G., and Whelan Porter, D., 2026. "aRTSjAM. A therapists' collective for embodied processing and being". In Frizell, C., and Rova, M. *Practice Research through Creative Bodies: Perspectives on Embodied Inquiry*. Routledge.

Butté, C., 2023. "Dancing at the Edge. Finding Home. Reflections on Movement Practice and Personal Loss". In *Body, Movement and Dance in Psychotherapy*, *18*(4): 305–315. https://doi.org/10.1080/17432979.2023.2268134.

Butté, C., and Colbert, T., eds., 2023. *Embodied Approaches to Supervision. The Listening Body*. Routledge.

Dickens, C., 2015. *The Uncommercial Traveller*. Oxford University Press.

Hayes, N., 2021. *The Book of Trespass*. Bloomsbury.

Le Guin, U., 2018. *The Left Hand of Darkness*. Gollancz.

Negueruela-Azarola, E., 2025. "It is about Time: Chronos/Kairos, Transformative Research and Learning and Development". *Language Teaching Research Quarterly*, *46*, 130–145. DOI: 10.32038/ltrq.2024.46.10.

Reeve, S., 2011. *Nine Ways of Seeing a Body*. Triarchy Press.

Solnit, R., 2001. *Wanderlust*. Verso.

Solnit, R., 2017. *A Field Guide to Getting Lost*. Canongate.

van Gennep, A., 1960. *The Rites of Passage*. The University of Chicago Press.

Concluding Thoughts

Anna Chesner, Céline Butté and Bryn Jones

The process of co-authoring this book has given us the opportunity to revisit and rediscover aspects of supervision and our thoughts around it. We have worked to hone several essential and purposeful questions which have fuelled our discussions. We have supported and challenged each other to determine what is necessary, superfluous and adequate to include. The dialogic process has given us a chance to clarify what we think and what we mean with the words we use. Coming from slightly different professional backgrounds this has been a lively and creative process in its own right and evocative of the supervisory process itself. Indeed, we have engaged all five supervisory roles in the process of our collaboration. The *administrative* task of creating our frame and structure has been supported by the engaged background presence of our publisher Routledge and particularly our editor Lauren Redhead. We have *facilitated* each other's thinking and articulation of our thoughts through discussion, listening, concretising ideas and having the courage to propose changes of tack. The role of *teacher* has passed between us as needed and has also been held by the project itself. Collaborating with Andrea Blair for the illustrations has certainly pushed us to be clear about what we mean and what is most pertinent to show. We have been *consultant* and *evaluator* for each other, recognising our individual complementary strengths and need for critique and support. Antony Williams introduces the concept of *Clinical Wisdom* in his book (Williams, 1995: 09). In writing this book we have attempted to hone our own *Creative and Supervisory Wisdom* and foster those qualities in the reader.

Every book is of its time. While we have integrated the world of online work as an optional norm within supervision practice and taken some steps outside of the consulting room, we recognise that we live in a time of massive change. We are now faced with the upsurge in the use of and interest in AI. The implication that this will have on safe professional and supervisory practice is yet to be discovered. It seems therefore important to stress here that safety within a specific coaching or supervisory relationship and frame is co-created by us as supervisors with our supervisees and is context specific. As the professional context changes, the need for reflection, respect for safe boundaries and creativity will continue to be crucial.

DOI: 10.4324/9781003435655-18

The therapist and supervisor Louis Zinkin once wrote an essay entitled Supervision: The Impossible Profession (Zinkin, 1995: 240). In it he grapples with the task from the alternating roles and perspectives of being both a supervisor and a supervisee. In considering this we are put in touch with the relational heart which feeds and sustains the life of the supervisory encounter. It reminds us again that the essence of supervision is collaborative and that from such creative and generative spaces, something seemingly impossible might become possible.

References

Williams, A., 1995. *Visual & Active Supervision.* Norton.
Zinkin, L., 1995. *Jungian Perspectives on Clinical Supervision.* Daimon.

The Creative Supervisor Toolkit

Figure T

This list is a prompt and guide for the creative supervisor. It can be adapted by the supervisor and sent to online supervisees. This gives them the option of having some of the basics to hand prior to their supervision sessions, allowing a smooth transition into whichever creative intervention is deemed suitable for their supervisory inquiry.

The Creative Supervisor Toolkit

Recommended resources for each method described in Part II:

Small World (Chapter 4)

Plain coloured cloth(s) for background.

Small objects such as stones and shells which are non-specific in meaning.

Figurines and small symbolic objects representing people, animals, buildings and everyday objects in miniature.

Ribbons, string and pegs to delineate boundaries.

Optional communicube/communiwell or small table.

Role Work (Chapter 5)

Chairs and cushions to locate each role in a separate space.

Plain coloured cloth to put empty chair into role or to drape on shoulder when using role online.

Four Elements (Group Supervision Approach, Chapter 7)

Six chairs, four on the stage and two at the side.

Chairs for relevant number of people in the audience.

Flip chart on stand.

Three to four pastels/felt pens.

A few plain coloured cloths.

Optional handheld musical instrument(s).

Cycle of Change (Group Supervision Approach, Chapter 7)

A large enough space for the group to move in.

Long lengths of different coloured cloths, sufficient to map out the mandala shape on the floor. Include spring, summer, autumn and winter colours.

Optional fans or other props that evoke the symbolism of the four seasons.

Six Shape Supervision Structure (6S) (Chapter 8)

Drawing paper, preferably A3.

Chalk and oil pastels, wax crayons, watercolour paints to allow less predictable mark-making and felt pens.

Hand wipes.

Seven Step Relationship Sequence (7SRS) (Chapter 9)

Plain cloth folded into letterbox shape.

Selection of image cards and postcards of your choice (approximately 25).

NB avoid cards with definitive meanings and names.

Mandala (Chapter 10)

Large piece of paper – preferably A3.
Chalk and oil pastels, wax crayons, watercolour paints to allow less predictable
   mark making and felt pens.
Hand wipes.
NB if using this method in group, a large enough space for all to move.

Framework for the Embodied Reflective Narrative (FERN) (Chapter 11)

Long lengths of wide coloured ribbon (2.5–10 cm) in two or three different colours
   to delineate the map on the floor.
Optional small objects to define the zones of Self, Relationship and Bigger Picture.

Creative Supervision Outdoors (Chapter 13)

First aid kit.
For online practice:
Optional: a second camera on a stand *gives the option of viewing both the made
   object and the face of the supervisee.*

Glossary

Aesthetic distance   the link between standing back, being separate from and the ability to have a clear perspective whilst viewing an aspect of self or practice. We invite aesthetic distance when we facilitate the supervisee to create a representation of an aspect of self or practice that can be viewed from outside.

Arc of the session   the tripartite structure, beginning with dialogue and finding a supervisory question, moving into the exploration of that question or focus including action methods as an option, and ending with final reflections.

Concretisation   this is the psychodramatic technique of marking a person or a concept with an object; for example, this object represents me, this next object represents my client, these other objects represent my clients' significant others, and these threads represent the lines of tension or attraction between them.

Cultural conserve   this Morenian concept refers to the mental and behavioural habits that can be useful shortcuts but which may inhibit our full creativity and spontaneity.

Deroling   the process of relinquishing the role of the other, moving back into one's own role. After a role reversal this involves returning to the physical place of your own role. In the case of projective techniques deroling is the process of withdrawing the projected meaning from an object; for example, this button no longer represents my client's mother. This involves returning the object to its original place in a box on a shelf.

Double   this is a psychodramatic term for speaking in the first person as the other, based on empathic attunement to their physicality. Psychologically, it is the lending of the supervisor's or fellow supervisee's ego to that of the supervisee. When someone receives a doubling statement, it is important they have the opportunity to accept, reject or adapt what has been offered in this way (see hygiene of the method).

Embodiment   Expression through the body, for example, embodying a role or a feeling. Also experiencing through the body and noticing what is happening at a somatic level/within the body.

Hygiene of the method   in literal terms this means facilitating a method 'cleanly', with clarity and attention to the dos and don'ts of each technique. Typically, this involves deroling what has been created, so that the arc of a session begins and ends in the dialogic space. It also involves appropriate languaging of the facilitation; for example, when doing Role Work it is important to give a direction rather than an invitation to reverse roles.

Interview-in-role   once a supervisee has taken on the role of a significant other, the conversation conducted with the supervisor begins with an interview-in-role. During this process the supervisee speaks in the first person as the client/colleague/significant other. The supervisor speaks to them in the second person, 'as if' they were the person of the role, rather than the supervisee (see hygiene of the method).

Mirror   this psychodramatic concept refers to the act of seeing something/ someone/oneself from the outside. It has links with aesthetic distance and facilitates reflective thinking.

Proxemics   the spatial relationships between objects and people. The concept highlights our sense of relational proximity or distance and is connected to Tele.

Role   the psychodramatic concept of a way of being, the functional form an individual takes at any moment. Also the technique of exploring through Role Work.

Role feedback   how it felt to hold a role. Typically, role feedback is given after deroling and in the past tense. For example, "When I was in role as your boss, I found myself feeling dismissive of you". It is also possible to ask for role feedback in a piece of group work where each person is invited to say what they are experiencing in the role. For example, "I am saying that I respect you, but I am feeling dismissive of what you are saying".

Role reversal   the psychodramatic technique of moving into the role of the other, taking on their posture, gestures, and ways of being in order to experience more closely their thoughts and to reproduce their words.

Role training   a specific use of Role Work in which the supervisee practises for a potential future situation, for example, a difficult conversation that needs to be had with a colleague or client. Role training offers the opportunity to make mistakes, exaggerate and try out different approaches without the consequences of doing it in real life.

Sculpt   this is the creation of a concretised image. In Small World the sculpt is in miniature, but concretisation allows us also to use larger objects in the space to map out a dynamic. We can also sculpt a situation by using other group members in the case of group supervision.

Sharing   a concept from psychodrama. After a piece of Role Work, once everyone has deroled, each person is invited to put into words their personal resonances or identification with elements of the work. To do this hygienically (see hygiene of the method) group members are encouraged to speak from the 'I' and to own their statements rather than to advise or interpret the work.

Sociodrama   one of Moreno's methods. Similar to psychodrama but taking social and community issues as its focus rather than the dynamics of an individual or group.

Sociometry   a scientific mapping of affinities, differences and resonances in a group. It relies on spatial relationships (proxemics) and groupings to make visible the underlying dynamics of any situation in that moment. Sociometry was developed by Moreno alongside psychodrama, sociodrama and group psychotherapy.

Subtext   a concept from theatre and literature, that which is communicated underneath the spoken words.

Supervisory question or focus   an agreed theme; this can be arrived at through dialogue between supervisor and supervisee. It might present itself as a necessary or urgent focus for the work from the outset of the session. It forms a mini-contract to attend to a specific enquiry or towards a specific outcome.

Tele   the psychodramatic term for the feeling charge between people. Tele can be subdivided into positive, negative or neutral and can be asymmetric or symmetric. Positive tele includes elements of admiration and identification. Negative tele might manifest as dislike, cautiousness or a desire for distance.

Witness   a technical term from Authentic Movement, a movement practice in which the participant is invited to pay attention both to what they are watching and the response of their own internal world.

Index

For Product Safety Concerns and Information please contact our EU
representative GPSR@taylorandfrancis.com
Taylor & Francis Verlag GmbH, Kaufingerstraße 24, 80331 München, Germany